FORGOTTEN
遗忘

Daniel York Loh

FORGOTTEN
遗忘

A new/old Chinese story in two acts

OBERON BOOKS
LONDON

WWW.OBERONBOOKS.COM

First published in 2018 by Oberon Books Ltd
521 Caledonian Road, London N7 9RH
Tel: +44 (0) 20 7607 3637 / Fax: +44 (0) 20 7607 3629
e-mail: info@oberonbooks.com
www.oberonbooks.com

PB ISBN: 9781786825032
E ISBN: 9781786825049

Cover image:
Concept © Emma Bailey
Photography © Suki Mok
Design © Emilie Chen

eBook conversion by Lapiz Digital Services, India.

10 9 8 7 6 5 4 3 2 1

'...by examining the past and revealing the future, I will show the path of progress to the people of the nation.'

Liang Qichao

Cast of Characters

OLD SIX
(20s)

BIG DOG
(20s)

SECOND MOON
GERMAN SOLDIER
MARIE
EMILIE TSCHENG
(20s)

EUNUCH LIN
THE FOLLOWER OF CHRIST
(around 20)

HEADMAN ZHANG
WILD SWAN
CORPSE
ARTIST
(40s)

PROFESSOR
LONGEVITY LIN
(20s)

Scene
China, France and between

Time
1917–1919

/ indicates overlapping dialogue

*Dedicated to the approximately 340,000
Chinese labourers who worked for the British,
French, Russian and American armies during
World War One, many of whom never managed
to return home.*

Act One

1. WEDGE: IN WHICH WE SEE ONE VERSION OF THE ENDING OF THE STORY

Somewhere in France on a battlefield in the mud.
OLD SIX with BIG DOG laid in front of him, dead. The sounds of explosions far off.

OLD SIX: *(Calling out.)* HEEEY!!!

CAN ANYBODY HEAR ME??? HEEEEY!!!

My friend…

My friend Big Dog…

Actually, I say 'friend,' but really I should say 'brother.'

Because we Chinese, in the Confucian ethos, tend to the familial with one another.

Everyone to us is an aunt or an uncle, first cousin or mother, grandpa or father, a sister or a brother.

So my brother Big Dog…

He was called 'Big Dog' because he was big and looked like a dog.

He got smashed to pieces by a mother-and-son cannon shell (we're even familial with weapons from hell) and now my brother Big Dog's guts have spilled out all over this trench and all over this battlefield and his celestial Confucian blood now mingles with that of the dead Western heroes who didn't know he was called Big Dog who couldn't tell us apart one from the other but now he's dead he's surely their brother too.

We can't leave, Big Dog. We can't leave…

(Sings.)

'Jingyang Ridge the way back home
Inn to rest, cure traveller's woes...'

During the above, unseen by OLD SIX, SECOND MOON has entered.
She is a bizarre sight. Dressed in an 'opera coat,' wearing a false
beard on her face to denote she is playing a man, with a baby strapped
to her stomach. Unlike OLD SIX, she is in full 'opera mode' – stylised
walking in a long circle around the stage, in 'character.'

SECOND MOON: *(Takes up the song.)*
    'Dark is the night and gone is the day
    From Magic Traveller we learn the Way'

OLD SIX: *(Seeing SECOND MOON, astonished.)* You!

SECOND MOON: *(As MIRACULOUS TRAVELLER.)* *'Pilgrim Wu*
    Song!'

OLD SIX: You can't be here!

SECOND MOON: *(As MIRACULOUS TRAVELLER.)* *'I travel the*
    circle of the stage, Pilgrim Wu Song.'

OLD SIX: But this is no stage!

SECOND MOON: *(As MIRACULOUS TRAVELLER.)* *'Wu Song the*
    Pilgrim –'

OLD SIX: No, I'm Old Six –

SECOND MOON: *(As MIRACULOUS TRAVELLER.)* *'– gallant*
    warrior of the marsh.'

OLD SIX: I'm no gallant warrior.

SECOND MOON: *(As MIRACULOUS TRAVELLER.)* *'You slay tigers,*
    kill whole armies, wield flashing swords/ deal death so harsh.'

OLD SIX: *(At the same time.)* No. No, I can't.

SECOND MOON: *(As MIRACULOUS TRAVELLER.) 'Rise up, brother! Come with me!'*

OLD SIX: The cannon shell killed Big Dog and broke my legs. I can't move.

SECOND MOON: *(As MIRACULOUS TRAVELLER.) 'You need but walk the circle, Pilgrim Wu Song.'*

OLD SIX: Back home?

SECOND MOON: *(Reciting.) 'The Miraculous Traveller leads you, pilgrim. We shall return to our fraternity home on the marsh.'*

OLD SIX: *(Dares to believe.) 'You have that marvellous ability to travel quickly, brother'.*

SECOND MOON: *(As if, even in a dream of an opera, her true self fights through.)* Hush now, my love. This life is like red dust on the wind.

BANG!

A huge but almost slow-motion explosion. BANG!

The stage is rocked by explosions. SECOND MOON takes OLD SIX's hand and he rises up along with BIG DOG, as they both travel the circle of the stage led by SECOND MOON, while drums and cymbals crash as the 'opera' commences...

OLD SIX and BIG DOG exit, leaving just SECOND MOON as MIRACULOUS TRAVELLER to introduce the drama –

SECOND MOON: *(As MIRACULOUS TRAVELLER.) 'I am the Miraculous Traveller. I can cross oceans and lands in the same time the sun will rise and fall. I wear magic talismans, eat no fowl or hog or hound or hare, let not wine touch my lips, travel 800 li a day like wind...'*

Drums, shrill pipe, cacophonous noise. Excited shouting...

2. IN WHICH WE MEET THE MAGICAL CHINESE VARIETY TROUPE OF HORSE SHOE VILLAGE

We are in Horse Shoe Village square. OLD SIX enters 'transformed.' They are in an 'opera.' BIG DOG has joined EUNUCH LIN. They both bang drums and clappers making the distinctive 'clack-clack-clack' Chinese theatre noise. Around them, watching, are assorted villagers, including HEADMAN ZHANG and LONGEVITY LIN.

ALL: *(Singing.)*
Jingyang Ridge the way back home
Inn to rest, cure traveller's woes
Dark is the night and gone is the day
From Magic Traveller we learn the Way'

OLD SIX: *(As PILGRIM WARRIOR.)* 'I am Wu Song. I'm a Qinghe County man! I'm also known as The Pilgrim. My parents died when I was young and I only have an elder brother (a real *elder brother).* One night I got drunk and punched a man so hard he died. So naturally I fled and took refuge with a fellow who invited me to join a gallant outlaw fraternity. But I'm worried about my elder brother, who I haven't heard from. So, along with the Miraculous Traveller here, I have journeyed to see Elder Brother Wu, arriving here at Jingyang Ridge, weary and tired from the mountains and lakes we have crossed...'

OLD SIX has seen HEADMAN ZHANG and hesitates to continue.

HEADMAN ZHANG: *(To OLD SIX from the 'audience.')* Carry on.

BIG DOG: *(As LANDLORD.)* 'I am the landlord here at Inn Of Three Bowls Do Not Cross Ridge.'

HEADMAN ZHANG: Stupid horse-face stack of meat.

LONGEVITY LIN laughs sycophantically.

EUNUCH LIN: *(As LANDLORD'S WIFE.)* 'I am Landlord's Wife here at Inn Of Three Bowls Do Not Cross Ridge.'

OLD SIX: *(As PILGRIM WARRIOR.)* 'Landlord, tell me. Why is your inn named Inn Of Three Bowls Do Not Cross Ridge?'

HEADMAN ZHANG: *(From the 'audience.')* Big Dog, you surly oaf. Think you can be an actor?

BIG DOG: *(As LANDLORD.)* 'Because, pilgrim, any disciple of Kao-Yan who drinks three bowls of my sweet wine will be far too drunk to walk back home across that ridge.'

HEADMAN ZHANG: The only thing you can pretend to be is a rat licking a cat's arse!

SECOND MOON: *(As MIRACULOUS TRAVELLER, hurriedly.)* 'Pilgrim Wu Song, I implore. It's truth he tells and our travel will impair, rest till day but drink no wine.'

HEADMAN ZHANG: *(To LONGEVITY LIN, loudly.)* I only watch this rustic menial hokum for Second Moon and her husband's sake.

LONGEVITY LIN: Honour and beauty can ask much from a strong man, Headman Zhang.

EUNUCH LIN: *(Under breath but too audibly.)* A flaccid man who eats too much, more like.

HEADMAN ZHANG: *(To EUNUCH LIN.)* I'd chop your balls off, boy. If you had any!

Roars with laughter as the crowd sycophantically laugh along.

EUNUCH LIN clacks his wood three times.

BIG DOG: *(As LANDLORD.)* 'Three bowls of my wine, Pilgrim. You'll be too drunk to stand.'

EUNUCH LIN: *(As LANDLORD'S WIFE.)* 'And a tiger dwells out on the ridge!'

SECOND MOON: *(As MIRACULOUS TRAVELLER.)* 'A tiger!!???!!!'

OLD SIX: *(As PILGRIM WARRIOR.) 'Three??? A mere three???'*

Accompanied by clacking wood and shrill pipe, OLD SIX (as the PILGRIM WARRIOR) downs one bowl of wine, then another, then another…

BIG DOG/EUNUCH LIN: *(In time with 'drinking.') 'Woooowah-hey! Woooowah-hey!'*

OLD SIX: *(As PILGRIM WARRIOR.) 'Three bowls of your mildew wine, landlord. And still I stand!'*

BIG DOG: *(As LANDLORD.) 'The like of which I never saw!'*

EUNUCH LIN: *(As LANDLORD'S WIFE.) 'This pilgrim is stout and strong!'*

OLD SIX: *(As PILGRIM WARRIOR.) 'I'm a Qinghe County man! More, you varlet! More!'*

SECOND MOON: *(As MIRACULOUS TRAVELLER.) 'Pilgrim, no!!!'*

OLD SIX downs more and more bowls, faster and faster –

BIG DOG/EUNUCH LIN: *(Faster in time with 'drinking.') 'Woooowah-hey! Woooowah-hey!'*

– rhythmically and percussively as the wood clacks and the cymbals crash, until –

OLD SIX: *(As PILGRIM WARRIOR.) 'Eighteen bowls! And now my head is light And now I will depart Into the wild dark night!'*

SECOND MOON: *(As MIRACULOUS TRAVELLER.) 'But… pilgrim…the tiger!'*

Silence.

HEADMAN ZHANG: Well???

What happens next??? Where's the tiger???

BIG DOG: Tomorrow at noon we continue our tale of the marsh, Headman Zhang.

HEADMAN ZHANG: You lousy son of a goblin's whore, how can you leave it there?

SECOND MOON: You know the tale, do you not, Headman Zhang?

OLD SIX: As every peasant does, you said.

HEADMAN ZHANG: I…you think in all my village duties and the taxes I must collect and the accounts I have to present at the chief magistrate's *yamen*…you think I have a cave in my head where this kind of twisted dick-piss lives?

Back to work then, those of you that can.

The crowd start to disperse, LONGEVITY LIN pauses to drop (very small) coins in OLD SIX's bowl.

LONGEVITY LIN: *(Grinning maliciously.)* Everything has beauty, but not everyone sees it. Keep practising, Old Six.

SECOND MOON: *(To OLD SIX – indicating her baby.)* He enjoyed performing with us, husband, but now the pig needs mucking out.

OLD SIX: And I was about to slay a tiger!

SECOND MOON: Pigs before tigers, husband. The order of nature and drama. *(To BIG DOG and EUNUCH LIN.)* You worked today?

BIG DOG: Red Eye said I ploughed the land too fast and left myself no work.

EUNUCH LIN: He said I was too weak to spread manure on his fields.

OLD SIX: When we all know our Eunuch Lin is as strong as an ox.

HEADMAN ZHANG: So you two scabby donkeys are just lazing around then?

BIG DOG: Unless you have work for us, Headman Zhang?

HEADMAN ZHANG: I wouldn't shit on you, Big Dog. Useless. Like your useless father before you.

OLD SIX: Peace, Headman Zhang. You'll spoil your spleen with this kind of bad talk. We look to you.

Beat.

HEADMAN ZHANG: Big Dog's foul face disturbs my bladder. And there I was, about to tell him something one of the foreign-man missionaries said. Old Six, I have village affairs to attend to. I will call on you shortly.

BIG DOG: What secret's this?

EUNUCH LIN: Headman Zhang, tell us!

HEADMAN ZHANG: Let's just say foreigners could be recruiting soon. They'll pay handsomely too. For any of you man enough. Live frugally, friends.   .

OLD SIX/SECOND MOON/BIG DOG/EUNUCH LIN: Go slowly, Headman Zhang.

HEADMAN ZHANG and LONGEVITY LIN exit.

OLD SIX: Foreigners?

BIG DOG: Fuck that.

OLD SIX: Why? There's nothing here.

BIG DOG: They've got big noses and they treat you like slaves.

EUNUCH LIN: It's just Headman Zhang's fart gas anyway.

OLD SIX: Come for dinner later, brothers? Wife, it's alright?

SECOND MOON: *(Referring to BIG DOG.)* The day he cuts that thing off the back of his head, he'll even get extra portions.

BIG DOG: That's my queue!

SECOND MOON: I know what it is!

BIG DOG: What's wrong with it?

SECOND MOON: It's so…Qing Dynasty!

OLD SIX: Come, wife, I must attend to the pig. That hapless creature is all our fortunes. *(To BIG DOG and EUNUCH LIN.)* At sundown.

EUNUCH LIN: Go slow.

BIG DOG: *(Deferentially.)* Sister-in-law.

SECOND MOON: Brother Dog.

Exit OLD SIX and SECOND MOON. BIG DOG waits till they're out of sight and immediately rummages in his bag, producing a pipe.

BIG DOG: I may have ploughed Red Eye's fields too fast for my own good but at least it paid me two silver dollars/

EUNUCH LIN: Where you buying that shit now?

BIG DOG: Japs are bringing it in.

He is lighting the pipe now.

Much more fun than those five-beating-one boring Germans.

EUNUCH LIN: That's why they have ten times as many soldiers here than the Germans did then?

BIG DOG: But the Germans had missionaries who beat us with sticks and sneered at our ways.

BIG DOG is now lying back as the opium hits him.

BIG DOG: We're just insects to these foreigners. Stay hidden from their sight and they won't be able to crush your bones.

Silence.

EUNUCH LIN: They're happy, aren't they?

BIG DOG: The foreigners are happy as a fat smiling Buddha that we're so weak and useless.

EUNUCH LIN: Not the foreigners, you pig's cock. I meant Old Six and Second Moon, who we must call our sister-in-law now.

BIG DOG: Most harmonious union. They're both good people. Blessings to them.

EUNUCH LIN: Big Dog?

BIG DOG: Eunuch Lin?

EUNUCH LIN: Do you think you'll marry?

BIG DOG: I was born on the fifteenth day of the seventh month. Who'd have me?

EUNUCH LIN: No one believes that shit anymore!

BIG DOG: This village is about as modern as your uncle's bamboo pole. They still believe I'm a wild ghost from a lotus lantern.

Sing me a song you miserable horse-face.

EUNUCH LIN sings softly, unaccompanied.

EUNUCH LIN: *(Singing.)*
'Will I know what love is
Will it light my door
Those who know what love is
Rare as summer snow
We poor are reckoned useful
When young and strong and hale
Weak and old we're cast aside
Like bones all stripped of brawn...'

The lights have faded and faded...

3. BIG DOG IS BRUTALLY PUNISHED FOR HIS
BAD HABITS BY HEADMAN ZHANG

Twilight. BIG DOG still slumbers in his opium stupor. EUNUCH LIN still sings softly to himself, the words no longer audible. Now subsides...

Silence as the sun sets...

Out of nowhere appear HEADMAN ZHANG and LONGEVITY LIN, armed with sticks.

CRACK!

HEADMAN ZHANG strikes BIG DOG with his stick.

HEADMAN ZHANG: Useless, shit-smoking, poison-sucking, dried-up old woman's backyard!

CRACK! Strikes him again.

Two hundred and fifty rice bucket plague god! You don't even want your face, you dumb egg!

CRACK! Now LONGEVITY LIN strikes BIG DOG, who has awakened sufficiently to cry in pain.

EUNUCH LIN: What are you doing? What are you doing?

HEADMAN ZHANG: *(To LONGEVITY LIN.)* Keep hold of this
female life-breath or by the deities I'll break his girlish back.

*LONGEVITY LIN grabs hold of EUNUCH LIN, while HEADMAN
ZHANG kicks the now prone BIG DOG in the stomach.*

Get up! Get up, you sawn-off bait for the executioner! Up!

BIG DOG climbs wearily and painfully to his feet.

EUNUCH LIN: Headman Zhang, in the name of Guanyin,
have mercy, Headman Zhang, I beg of you, please,
be kind/

HEADMAN ZHANG: Remains of a peach, be silent!

To BIG DOG, who is now standing, in pain.

Well?

BIG DOG: Well what?

HEADMAN ZHANG: Where's your pipe, coffin bait?

BIG DOG: What pipe?

HEADMAN ZHANG: Release your mother's fart gas, fool,
everyone knows you smoke that shit.

BIG DOG: I stopped!

HEADMAN ZHANG: You're stopping now, running dog, give
me that pipe or I'll beat this glass friend of yours so badly
the only song he'll be singing will be of the eighteen levels
of hell.

BIG DOG: It's there, it's over there…my bag.

HEADMAN ZHANG: *(To LONGEVITY LIN.)* Get it.

EUNUCH LIN: Headman Zhang, I don't understand. What is
it to you?

HEADMAN ZHANG: How would a swarthy weakling like you understand? Times are changing. They want this place cleaned up from all the good-for-nothing filth-doing that's been the custom in these parts for too long. Means this –

Holds up pipe.

– is trouble for me –

Breaks pipe across his knee.

– means I won't tolerate it anymore. Our new Republic wants fit men. This village needs fit men/

BIG DOG: Why? There's no work to be done. The fields are either arid or flooded into oblivion. What use are workers when there's nothing to work?

HEADMAN ZHANG: Whether you're of use or not is piss in wind. You're a blot on my record, you quail pigeon.

But your luck may be changing. Your friend and his good wife are expecting you for dinner, yes? I've just delivered them some news. Take your southern customer here *(indicates EUNUCH LIN)* and get up there now.

Nods at LONGEVITY LIN, who releases EUNUCH LIN, and they start to move off.

EUNUCH LIN: How?

BIG DOG: I'm alright. The peace smoke filled my body with harmony.

HEADMAN ZHANG: *(Turning back.)* The new Republic needs you fit, Big Dog. I catch you with this shit again –

Holds up broken pipe.

– it'll be your head I'll break. Fucking cheap goods!

Exit HEADMAN ZHANG and LONGEVITY LIN. We hear the sound of SECOND MOON singing…

4. THE WAR IN THE WEST PRESENTS OPPORTUNITIES THAT ARE WEIGHED UP IN THE EAST

The home of OLD SIX and SECOND MOON. Small, cramped, dingy. Dominated by pots, pans and heavy wooden buckets. SECOND MOON is singing to her child, who she carries.

SECOND MOON: *(Singing.)*
'Mulberry leaves upon our doorstep
Tell of winter's chill
God of nature, 'low our portion
Upon your mercy still
Child of mine, are you our fortune
Bringing blessings from afar
Luck we long for, luck that burgeons
Light our way oh lonely star…'

During the song, OLD SIX has entered. There is an awkward silence between them.

SECOND MOON: The part where the Pilgrim Warrior slays the tiger. It shouldn't be so heroic.

Men aren't brave. They're just foolish.

OLD SIX: Wife, there is no choice.

SECOND MOON: There is choice in abundance!

OLD SIX: The land won't yield. One more flood (which Geomancer Wu is predicting) and we'll be in famine/ all over again –

SECOND MOON: Geomancer Wu is drunk on sack wine and passes wind in his talk/

OLD SIX: He's not been wrong these past five seasons/

SECOND MOON: He knows bad news will have people running for miles for his services, good news only makes us sleep/

OLD SIX: We'll starve!

Don't you see? It's more money than I can make here. Yourself and my son will be cared for financially.

Headman Zhang may well be un/couth and rough –

SECOND MOON: You're like a well-natured mountain tortoise/ with a soft shell!

OLD SIX: – but even bandits fear him/as tiger cubs fear a dragon –

SECOND MOON: Trusting in headmen and geomancers like a dull-minded peasant with no ounce of good judgement in/ you!

OLD SIX: Wife, this country of ours is on its knees!/

SECOND MOON: And you think you can put it back on its feet by kowtowing to/ foreigners?

OLD SIX: The foreigners will respect us more if we help/ them in their w–

SECOND MOON: Foreigners take and take and take and then they take some more. Will you never l–

BIG DOG and EUNUCH LIN have entered during this. Awkward silence.

SECOND MOON: Welcome, welcome.

EUNUCH LIN: We can go if it's no/ longer convenient.

OLD SIX: Come in/ come in.

SECOND MOON: No/ please, sit.

BIG DOG: We don't want to/ trouble our brother and sister-in-law.

EUNUCH LIN: We can always go and eat/ Old Crow's sweet potatoes.

OLD SIX: You're no trouble/ at all.

BIG DOG: Old Crow will sell to us/ cheaply.

SECOND MOON: *(Decisively.)* Please! Sit. The soup is ready.

BIG DOG: Very/ well then.

EUNUCH LIN: You're well?

OLD SIX: Yes, yes. Yourself?

BIG DOG: Our lateness. No face. My apologies.

EUNUCH LIN: Headman Zhang de/tained us.

BIG DOG: We were…talking/

EUNUCH LIN: Yes/

BIG DOG: With our Headman.

OLD SIX: About?

BIG DOG: …

EUNUCH LIN: Theatre/

BIG DOG: Theatre. He was giving his thoughts. On our/ performance.

OLD SIX: That it's too crude and clumsy to earn money outside this village?

SECOND MOON: That man is your drama master now?

OLD SIX: He knows what he knows.

SECOND MOON: That you're easily gulled.

I'll get the soup. *(To BIG DOG.)* A haircut would change your fortunes. Maybe even the fortunes of the entire village.

Exit SECOND MOON.

BIG DOG: *(Calling after her.)* How do you know my queue hasn't protected this village these last twenty-five moons?

OLD SIX: She likes to chide, my wife.

EUNUCH LIN: She was always spirited.

OLD SIX: Headman Zhang told you then?

EUNUCH LIN: About what?

OLD SIX: The foreigners' war.

EUNUCH LIN: They have a war?

BIG DOG: Who cares? There's always foreigners fucking around here. Foreigners are pigs that play in shit and our Middle Country *is* their shit.

OLD SIX: Well, now they have a war. A big war.

EUNUCH LIN: With who?

OLD SIX: Each other.

BIG DOG: Here?

OLD SIX: In the West.

EUNUCH LIN: They fight each other?

BIG DOG: Jap bastards just drove the German bastards out, didn't they? Before that the Jap bastards beat the Russian bastards here. In China.

EUNUCH LIN: That's yellow foreigners against pale foreigners. I didn't know the big noses fight each other.

OLD SIX: Well, the big noses are fighting now.

BIG DOG: What's it got to do with us?

Unseen, SECOND MOON has returned.

SECOND MOON: They've killed so many of their own race
they want to transport our people there and kill them
as well.

BIG DOG: Second Mo– sister-in-law, my language, I/ apologise.

OLD SIX: Wife, Big Dog and Brother Eunuch/ need the plain
facts –

SECOND MOON: The foreigners need some dull stupid
peasants to stand in between them and get cut to pieces by
whatever savagery they've invented now/

EUNUCH LIN: They want us to fight with/ them?

OLD SIX: No, not fight, just work/

BIG DOG: But we'll be soldiers?

OLD SIX: In a way/

EUNUCH LIN: With uni/forms?

SECOND MOON: Smartly dressed in Western uniforms only
to be/ butchered on the battlefields –

OLD SIX: They'll pay ten silver dollars a month. There's
money to live on over…there. But ten silver dollars gets
sent here. With money you can reach even the gods. Our
families will be cared for here and we can return to a new
and better future with a country that's proud again, after
we have earned the respect of the good foreigners by
helping them defeat a tyrannous enemy.

EUNUCH LIN: Who's tyrannous? Whose side are we on?

OLD SIX: There's a group of them/

SECOND MOON: He doesn't even know!

OLD SIX: Of course I know, wife, we would be working for the British and they are in partnership with...others/

SECOND MOON: Such knowledge!

EUNUCH LIN: And who are the tyrants?

OLD SIX: The Germans.

BIG DOG: I can't tell them apart/

EUNUCH LIN: Are the Germans any worse than the rest?

OLD SIX: Yes! That's why the British and...the good foreigners are fighting them. The Germans want to take over the world/

SECOND MOON: Unlike the rest of them!

OLD SIX: Wife, you wouldn't know!

SECOND MOON: And neither would you!

EUNUCH LIN: I'll go.

Why not? If it's a choice between seeing their Western world and staying here starving, watching Big Dog get beaten by Headman Zhang, I'd rather try something new.

I'll go. If they'll take a eunuch.

OLD SIX: You work hard, they'll surely take you/

SECOND MOON: Dull-eyed stupidity/

EUNUCH LIN: Ten silver dollars!

OLD SIX: Big Dog?

EUNUCH LIN: Brother Dog, your teeth are falling out and you barely have clothes.

BIG DOG: I don't like it.

SECOND MOON: Someone here has some sense!

BIG DOG: I don't understand this 'good foreigners/bad foreigners' reasoning. We're all the same to them and they're all the same to me. Indeed all powerful creatures are the same to me. Monstrous/ clumsy beasts.

OLD SIX: Why did Headman Zhang beat you, Big Dog?

BIG DOG: He doesn't like my acting.

OLD SIX: Liar!

EUNUCH LIN: Headman Zhang beat Big Dog for smoking opium.

OLD SIX: I knew it!

BIG DOG: *(To EUNUCH LIN.)* Traitor!

OLD SIX: He only tells what the whole/ village knows –

EUNUCH LIN: You've been in love with the pipe for years/ now, Big Dog.

BIG DOG: So what if I have? My own cure for my own problems/

OLD SIX: And this is a cure. A chance to escape the pointless karma you live in and do something worthwhile. Your cousin can keep the money for you. When you return/–

BIG DOG: *If* I return/

OLD SIX: – you can even farm your own land. And we'll practice our variety show and tour the county for/ money.

EUNUCH LIN: We'll return, Big Dog. We're magical Chinese, the foreigners can't murder us.

BIG DOG: That's what the Boxers thought/

EUNUCH LIN: The Boxers were stupid ignorant hog-face peasants. We're a magical theatre troupe. The foreign devils will be entranced by our music and performance and line our path back to Shandong with gold and cherry blossoms.

OLD SIX: We won't be in the battle itself, Big Dog, the foreigners guarantee/ it.

BIG DOG: How the fuck do they guarantee that (apologies, Second Moon)? I watched the German big noses being driven out of Qingdao by the yellow-bowl Japanese dwarves and, believe me when I say, it was a terrifying sight to behold.

OLD SIX: We may not be blown to pieces here but we'll be starved into the next life like timid mice being drowned by rainfall in a ditch. I vote for firm action to put food in our bellies and our land on its feet.

EUNUCH LIN: *(To BIG DOG.)* Come with us, big brother.

Beat.

BIG DOG: It's reaching into a tiger's mouth to pull a tooth. I stay.

SECOND MOON: The dog has sense where men don't, it seems.

OLD SIX: Our little theatre troupe won't be the same without you. Already we'll be without sister-in-law Second/ Moon.

BIG DOG: You'll return. I'll light incense for your fortune every day/

EUNUCH LIN: When do we go?

OLD SIX: They're recruiting now. We should go quick before the foreigners change their mind.

SECOND MOON: Where must you go?

OLD SIX: Weihaiwei.

EUNUCH LIN: What the fuck's that (apologies, sister-in-law)?

OLD SIX: It's...a British place/

BIG DOG: As opposed to a Jap bullies' place or a Russian bullies'/ place –

OLD SIX: Headman Zhang knows/

SECOND MOON: Of course he knows/

OLD SIX: He is taking a cart tomorrow. At the fifth watch.

EUNUCH LIN: I have no bag.

OLD SIX: *(Looks around the small hut.)* Wife, where is my old sack?

SECOND MOON: The barn outside.

OLD SIX: *(To EUNUCH LIN.)* Come with me.

EUNUCH LIN: Kind thanks, Brother Six.

Exit OLD SIX and EUNUCH LIN.

Silence.

SECOND MOON: You!

BIG DOG: What?

SECOND MOON: Opium, pigtails. You're like a relic from a forgotten era.

BIG DOG: I'm traditional.

SECOND MOON: Only tradition lasts forever.

BIG DOG: Your husband's right though. There's nothing for me here.

SECOND MOON: That's not/ true –

BIG DOG: You're kind to me, sister. You always were.

SECOND MOON: Dogs deserve kindness. Especially abandoned ones.

BIG DOG: When we were children, you were kind to me then. I was a big clumsy oaf. And you were Sister Second Moon.

Always Sister Second Moon. Now you're married to my friend. Our friend. And I have to address you as 'sister-in-*law*.' As I knew I'd have to. But it sits strangely on my tongue.

SECOND MOON: Our lives are like flower petals floating on a fast stream.

BIG DOG: May I know…forgive my rudeness. It's wrong of me to ask, I should be beaten again, I have the manners of a dog as well/ as the name.

SECOND MOON: Geomancer Wu told my parents we were well-suited. Brother Six is a good man. As we both know.

Silence.

Enter OLD SIX and EUNUCH LIN with a tatty sack.

EUNUCH LIN: Big Dog, look at this! I'm ready for my travels now.

BIG DOG: Indeed you are.

OLD SIX: This is only temporary, little brother Eunuch. We'll buy you a new bag made of finest foreign leather from the wages you/ earn.

EUNUCH LIN: They make better leather in the Western world?

OLD SIX: Everything is better there. We Chinese are a low species. But we work hard and we learn quickly. And we can take the foreigners' skills and knowledge and make them our own.

EUNUCH LIN: And entertain them with our songs and dramas?

OLD SIX: They won't understand us.

EUNUCH LIN: They'll be bewitched by our tunes and soulful rendition. A story is not a literal thing that only people of a certain time and place and tongue can comprehend. A story is a mad thing that travels oceans and mountains and captures the hearts and minds of men and women from far far away. It can build peace between our peoples and earn us their regard and goodwill.

OLD SIX: It can, Eunuch Lin, it can. Even the grumpy dog agrees.

BIG DOG: I do.

EUNUCH LIN: My heart is so full tonight. I only regret that my brother Big Dog doesn't travel this journey of the Monkey King with us. The long road won't be the same…

Overcome, EUNUCH LIN begins to weep.

…the parting of our family is a terrible thing. The stars may be dim or bright but my brother and my sister-in-law will live inside me always.

OLD SIX: Hush now, little Eunuch, you'll move us all to tears.

BIG DOG: But you should dry them now.

I'm coming.

OLD SIX: Big Dog?

EUNUCH LIN: You're going/ to –

BIG DOG: Who else can play the clown in the drama?

OLD SIX: Brother Dog, this/ is too good.

EUNUCH LIN: My brother! My/ brother's coming!

SECOND MOON: Big Dog???

BIG DOG: *(To SECOND MOON.)* I'll bring him home. I promise
you. No harm will befall your husband while I'm by
his side.

EUNUCH LIN: Big Dog is coming!

BIG DOG: And when we return we'll be famous opera
performers.

OLD SIX: Brother, you bless us with your com/pany –

EUNUCH LIN: I will dance so finely for you, Big Dog,
you wait!

BIG DOG: Your dancing is as fine as the mountain spirit,
Eunuch Lin. Now we should prepare. The fifth watch, did
you say? I must go home and make ready/

EUNUCH LIN: I'll walk with you/ big brother.

BIG DOG: Headman Zhang's cart then?

OLD SIX: Headman Zhang's cart to Weihaiwei and then the
wide world beyond.

BIG DOG: I can't wait to see the look on that freshwater
turtle's face when he sees me going off to the war!

EUNUCH LIN: The old toad will shit his arsehole in shock (apologies, sister-in-law).

BIG DOG: Say goodbye now, little clown-dancer.

EUNUCH LIN: Goodbye, sister-in-law.

SECOND MOON: Don't waste your best acting on the comedy courtesan characters, brother Eunuch. Save it for the moments of real drama.

EUNUCH LIN: I will, sister, I promise. *(To OLD SIX.)* Tomorrow, brother!

OLD SIX: Tomorrow.

BIG DOG: *(To SECOND MOON. This is difficult.)* My sister and my friend. May heaven bestow on you the blessings a lowly man like myself is unable to.

Beat.

SECOND MOON: *(With huge feeling.)* Goodbye, Brother Dog. Perform with fire always.

BIG DOG abruptly turns away.

BIG DOG: *(Decisively.)* Eunuch Lin, let's go. *(To OLD SIX.)* Tomorrow, brother.

OLD SIX: Tomorrow. Go slowly.

EUNUCH LIN: Goodbye.

Exit BIG DOG and EUNUCH LIN.

SECOND MOON and OLD SIX face each other in silence as the singing men in the recruitment area invade the scene and SECOND MOON vanishes...

5. AT THE RECRUITING CENTRE BIG DOG
GETS A HAIRCUT AND EUNUCH LIN PASSES THE TEST

*We are in the waiting area for Chinese Labour Corps (CLC) volunteers
to be checked and examined. OLD SIX and EUNUCH LIN sing to the
accompaniment of EUNUCH LIN's drum and OLD SIX's pipe while
HEADMAN ZHANG watches on, as does the man we will come to know
as THE PROFESSOR.*

MEN: *'From the far far west*
We hear a far-off song
From even further than the quest
Of our tricksy Wu Kong
We hear the angry tune
With a fractured refrain
Of guns and dragoons
Beating time with chicane
Angry Europeans
They crossed over our land
With their railways and buildings
So mighty and so grand
Hungry for resources
Like dragons at the door
We serve angry Europeans
In their hungry angry war'

HEADMAN ZHANG: If you addlepated bumpkins work as
hard as you sing, you'll make our new republic proud.

EUNUCH LIN: What is a republic anyway?

HEADMAN ZHANG: Never you mind, cheap goods, just get in
line and do what/ you're told.

PROFESSOR: A republic is intended to be a sovereign state
or country organised with a form of government in which
power resides in elected individuals representing the
citizen body.

I say 'intended' because our government more resembles a squabbling band of smooth-faced children who take turns to sulk in their provincial hideaways.

They all turn to look at THE PROFESSOR, HEADMAN ZHANG with some suspicion.

HEADMAN ZHANG: Don't strain yourself on this flute player's bullshit, friend. He didn't come here to find out about politics. Little worm's too thick to understand anyway.

PROFESSOR: You're not though, sir?

HEADMAN ZHANG: Not what?

PROFESSOR: Perhaps you can enlighten us all as to the differences between a monarchy, a constitutional monarchy (which some still contest would be for the better) and an outright republic, which I certainly believe we should rest our hopes with?

OLD SIX: What were we before?

EUNUCH LIN: The Great Qing Empire. We had an Emperor chosen by Heaven/

PROFESSOR: Superstitious primitive half-deck. The Emperor of the Middle Kingdom was the god's stick put in place by murder and scheming ambition –

OLD SIX: He's right/

PROFESSOR: – and in the case of the 'Great' Qing, our Son of Heaven was a Manchu/ conqueror.

HEADMAN ZHANG: Wait wait wait.

You mean we haven't got an emperor anymore?

Beat. Then the rest burst into laughter.

How was I supposed to know?

More laughter.

OLD SIX: You work for our leaders do you not?

HEADMAN ZHANG: Why do you think our village survives as it does? Because I know how to sweep my own doorstep.

PROFESSOR: This is why a Frenchman once described us Chinese as a sleeping dragon.

OLD SIX: Headman Zhang is a mighty dragon indeed.

EUNUCH LIN: And he certainly sleeps sound/ly!

HEADMAN ZHANG: So what's happened to the Emperor now then?

PROFESSOR: They just attempted to restore him/ actually –

EUNUCH LIN: You mean –?

PROFESSOR: A dynasty that came and went like a fleeting breeze.

HEADMAN ZHANG: *(Suspiciously.)* You talk like some sort of oracle bone.

PROFESSOR: *(To HEADMAN ZHANG.)* Merely a candidate for recruitment like yourself.

HEADMAN ZHANG: Well, that's/ not –

EUNUCH LIN: Headman Zhang's not/ volunteering –

OLD SIX: As the Headman of our village he has to stay. Don't you, Headman Zhang?

HEADMAN ZHANG: I'm too old. My calves aren't what they were.

PROFESSOR: The path's still open, friend. They want as many as possible and there'll be a few failing here,/ believe me.

HEADMAN ZHANG: No, no, I leave this for the young colts/

PROFESSOR: And you don't believe the young colts should learn something about whose interests they'll be serving when they sign up?

HEADMAN ZHANG: …

They're peasants with hairy balls. They dig shit and pull carts. What do they need to know?

Enter BIG DOG. He has short hair and now wears a rough uniform.

EUNUCH LIN: Big Dog!!!

OLD SIX: You look like/–

BIG DOG: *(In shock.)* They cut off my queue!

HEADMAN ZHANG: He looks like a shaved nun!

BIG DOG: My queue! My pigtail! They chopped it off.

EUNUCH LIN: Brother Dog, you're as castrated as me now!

VOICE: *(Off.)* Next! Next! Let's keep it moving now.

Another of the men exits into the 'recruitment area.'

OLD SIX: What happened, Big Dog?

EUNUCH LIN: What did they make you do?

BIG DOG: They wanted to know my name.

EUNUCH LIN: Amitabha Buddha!

BIG DOG: *(Rapidly.)* It's true. So I say, 'I don't know.' They say, 'What do you mean you don't know, of course you know, it's your name,' I say, 'I don't know my name. From as far back as I can remember everyone in my family called me Big Dog because I was big and looked like a dog,' so they say 'So what's your *family name*?' I say, 'I don't know, I just called them mum and dad,' and they say, 'So what did everyone else call them?' I said, 'Farm Worker' and 'Farm Worker's Wife.' They said, 'Did anyone ever call them Mr and Mrs something, like Mr and Mrs Lin or something?' I said, 'Yes, I think that was it, how did you know?' They said, 'The last fellow was called Lin,' I said, 'Well, everyone in my village is either called Lin or Zhang (that I know of anyway) so I reckon that must be it,' so they wrote something on here. *(Indicates his metal wristband.)* What does it say?

OLD SIX: Headman Zhang?

HEADMAN ZHANG: Where do I have time to learn that shit?

EUNUCH LIN: I fuck!

OLD SIX: We'll never know.

THE PROFESSOR has grabbed BIG DOG's arm and reads his wristband.

PROFESSOR: It says 'Lin Son Of The Hairy Dog.'

BIG DOG: What the f–??

OLD SIX: Never mind never mind, what else?

BIG DOG: Spent the longest time looking in my eyes?

HEADMAN ZHANG: Trying to find your brains!

PROFESSOR: Trachoma.

EUNUCH LIN: What?

PROFESSOR: It's a disease that affects the eyelids. If it isn't treated it leads to blindness.

EUNUCH LIN: Physician Wang knows how to cure it.

OLD SIX: You think the foreigners will allow Physician Wang to come and spread baby's piss on your eye and make you drink rhino horn extract?

PROFESSOR: It spreads quickly. Clothing, flies. They don't want it contaminating their soldiers.

EUNUCH LIN: It's common amongst us rough peasants?

PROFESSOR: Poor hygiene.

BIG DOG: Hyg...

OLD SIX: What next, Brother Dog?

BIG DOG: Sprayed me with water, gave me these clothes and clipped this thing on my wrist/

EUNUCH LIN: They made you take your clothes off?

BIG DOG: Then sprayed me with water. Cold as the second court of hell it was.

EUNUCH LIN: They'll see I'm...

OLD SIX: Maybe they won't/

HEADMAN ZHANG: You think foreigners don't know balls when they don't see them?

BIG DOG: Maybe they won't look.

OLD SIX: Maybe they won't care.

HEADMAN ZHANG: Those mighty big noses won't want a smooth-crotch bunny in their/ army.

PROFESSOR: Some of the finest soldiers in the old imperial armies were eunuchs. Commanded thousands of men and won battles and the favour of emperors.

BIG DOG: There you go, brother Lin.

SHOUT: *(Off.)* Next!

BIG DOG: *(To EUNUCH LIN.)* Go next. Get it over with.

OLD SIX: Courage, little brother.

HEADMAN ZHANG: They'll see he *has* no little brother. Ha ha ha!

EUNUCH LIN exits.

OLD SIX: You think they'll take him?

PROFESSOR: They seem more concerned about eyes and strength, though the foreigners may find it bizarre.

HEADMAN ZHANG: You mean their foreign kings don't have fairy boys to look after all their concubines?

PROFESSOR: They don't have concubines. Officially.

OLD SIX: *(To THE PROFESSOR.)* Where are you from, friend?

PROFESSOR: Zhili province.

BIG DOG: You speak our dialect so well.

PROFESSOR: My mother was from your parts.

OLD SIX: What's your name?

PROFESSOR: /

OLD SIX: I'll never be able to pronounce a name in a strange dialect. We'll just call you 'Professor.'

PROFESSOR: As you wish.

BIG DOG: Professor's good with me.

OLD SIX: You're not a peasant like ourselves, though?

PROFESSOR: I'm a teacher.

HEADMAN ZHANG: What are you doing here then? This is work for low-menial bumpkins.

PROFESSOR: I'm not afraid of hard work. Plus I need to know. Don't you?

BIG DOG: Need to know what?

PROFESSOR: Have you never ever wondered why they're so far ahead of us? Why they're so small yet so strong? Whilst we're so large but weak? Three quarters of our land here is controlled by foreign powers who gnaw away at us like caterpillars on a great leaf. These foreigners live inside legations where they have their own laws. One of them can kill you dead now and not stand trial here. They charge us indemnities for having the temerity to be defeated by them in wars because we wouldn't buy their opium. To help us out they lend us money to repay those indemnities but charge us punitive interest leaving us as financially impaired as a blind beggar in the market/

HEADMAN ZHANG: Even the spirits cannot fathom this one's talk.

BIG DOG: I understood the part about/ opium.

PROFESSOR: There are four hundred million of us! We can't read, we can't write and we speak so many different languages we can't even talk to each other. The foreigners have a simple writing system which any of their people can master. We communicate in arcane pictograms designed to keep our people ignorant and base. We could have carried on for another millennium dreaming the dreams of tortoises. But the rest of the world came calling and here we were. A humiliated backwater.

Enter EUNUCH LIN, looking shocked and traumatised, in a uniform.

OLD SIX: Eunuch Lin!

BIG DOG: Little brother!

PROFESSOR: What happened?

EUNUCH LIN: They…they…

OLD SIX: Tell us, Eunuch Lin.

HEADMAN ZHANG: I'll whip your southern customer arsehole all the way back to Horse Shoe Village/

BIG DOG: No, Headman Zhang, he's in a uni/form.

EUNUCH LIN: They didn't even look!

EUNUCH LIN holds up his wristband.

BIG DOG: Fucking Wu Song's sword!

HEADMAN ZHANG: You're a Taoist magician, boy!

OLD SIX: You did it!

PROFESSOR: Congratulations, Eunuch Lin!

BIG DOG: The opera survives!

OLD SIX: Wait, *I* haven't been in yet.

BIG DOG: A formality, Brother Six/

EUNUCH LIN: If they'll take me they'll surely take you/

PROFESSOR: You look healthy enough to me/

HEADMAN ZHANG: These foreigners will even take a glass warrior!

VOICE: *(Off.)* Next!

BIG DOG: *(To OLD SIX.)* Good fortune, brother.

And now the lights fade on all except OLD SIX, who steps forward to a presence we don't see, removes his clothes, is sprayed with water, is towelled down and begins to don his 'army style' clothes...

SINGING: *(Off.)*
'Awaken to emptiness
Awaken to toil
Those angry Europeans
Will make war for their spoils'

Now he turns, dressed in army 'uniform.'

An unseen foreign presence ushers OLD SIX into a line with BIG DOG, EUNUCH LIN and THE PROFESSOR.

Instructed from out front, they pose awkwardly. Are made to adjust their uniforms. They pose again, either trying to look like the perceived notion of stoic dutiful Chinese workers or grinning cheesily like happy grateful peasants –

SNAP!

They are momentarily blinded by the flash. They are then ordered to move off as we hear the sound of a train as the men 'travel.'

OLD SIX turns one last time but doesn't quite see his wife, SECOND MOON, who moves into view along with HEADMAN ZHANG, as OLD SIX disappears along with the rest...

6. IN WHICH THE HEADMAN OF THE VILLAGE MAKES AN OFFER OF HELP TO A WIFE LEFT ON HER OWN

OLD SIX's small dwelling in Horse Shoe Village. SECOND MOON and HEADMAN ZHANG.

HEADMAN ZHANG: In another life you'd be an emperor's consort, Old Six's wife.

SECOND MOON: Bound feet hold no appeal for me.

HEADMAN ZHANG: You trip the waves better without.

SECOND MOON: I play the Miraculous Traveller after all.

HEADMAN ZHANG: He's like a son to me, you know. Your husband. Both of you…I hold here. *(Taps his heart.)*

SECOND MOON: Our headman is like a father to all in/ this village.

HEADMAN ZHANG: No children of my own, see.

SECOND MOON: Headman Zhang's benevolence and dedication to our people knows no boun/dary –

HEADMAN ZHANG: She died in childbirth. My/ wife –

SECOND MOON: I recall.

HEADMAN ZHANG: Just solitude since. Like a cold embrace in the second level of hell.

SECOND MOON: Circumstance was unkind to you, Headman Zhang.

HEADMAN ZHANG: *(Dismissively.)* Just my five-element fate.

SECOND MOON: I never expected my husband to travel to the land of foreign giants.

HEADMAN ZHANG: I tried to persuade him not to, you know. Didn't seem right to abandon you and the child.

SECOND MOON: Heaven brings nothing to our door so we must search for it. It's been the way of generations past and I'm sure will be so for/ all the ones to come.

HEADMAN ZHANG: *(Referring to the cradle.)* Talking of which. The boy there. Is he well?

SECOND MOON: I'm preparing millet porridge for him now.

HEADMAN ZHANG: That's good. That's good.

Awkward silence.

SECOND MOON: Well/ then –

HEADMAN ZHANG: I was –

Apologies. I'm like an unfettered colt.

SECOND MOON: No, no. I would not dream to interrupt our beneficent headman.

Beat.

HEADMAN ZHANG: I know it's hard for you. With no husband. I can…help you.

SECOND MOON: You're too generous, Headman Zhang. I'm sure, if there's anything, I won't hesitate to call on you.

HEADMAN ZHANG: Your husband's pay. You must collect it from Weihaiwei.

SECOND MOON: He told his brother.

HEADMAN ZHANG: On the fifth day of each lunar moon.

SECOND MOON: I was given directions/

HEADMAN ZHANG: I can take you in the cart.

SECOND MOON: Headman Zhang's generosity flows over our village like a waterfall of bounteous joy. But we must have a care to be frugal/ with it.

HEADMAN ZHANG: I can be a good friend to you, Second Moon. If you'll allow me. Be a good friend to me. This floating world is a lonely place. The fifth day of the month. I will come then.

SECOND MOON: Thank you, Headman Zhang.

HEADMAN ZHANG: Till then. Daughter-in-law.

He pauses as he leaves.

All these pots and pans you have. My house is bare and barren. No woman's touch.

Exit HEADMAN ZHANG.

SECOND MOON is alone. The child cries.

At the same time we hear a man moaning in agony from the other side of the world –

7. HISTORY AND GEOGRAPHY LESSONS AND WHAT ABDICATION OF EMPERORS MEANS TO ONE BOY IN A RURAL VILLAGE

BIG DOG: AAAAAOOOOORRRRRRGGGGGGHHHHH!

We are in the hold of a ship. OLD SIX and EUNUCH LIN squat near THE PROFESSOR. BIG DOG is curled up on the floor in some discomfort but is nevertheless attentive.

PROFESSOR: They believed their territory was being stolen or some such/

EUNUCH LIN: So they killed this Archduke foreigner?

PROFESSOR: They did.

OLD SIX: And this Archduke foreigner's father took revenge?

PROFESSOR: No, this Archduke foreigner's father didn't like his son.

BIG DOG: *(Holding his stomach.)* Why not?

EUNUCH LIN: Brother Big Dog, try to rest/

BIG DOG: There's no rest for me, keep talking, Professor/

OLD SIX: *(To PROFESSOR.)* Our brother Big Dog sucked the last of his poison/ yesterday.

BIG DOG: *(Mock theatrical.)* Farewell to the pipe, farewell to my love/

EUNUCH LIN: *(To THE PROFESSOR.)* He'll be of some discomfort for a/ day or two.

BIG DOG: Continue with the foreign devil story, Professor, it distracts my agonised senses.

PROFESSOR: I only say what I read in the newspapers but I believe it was a case of honour.

BIG DOG: Only the truly powerful will indulge themselves with honour.

PROFESSOR: Indeed you're correct, oh sickly Big Dog.

The Austrian-Hungarian foreigners/–

EUNUCH LIN: Who have an emperor/

PROFESSOR: Correct – issued an ultimatum which the Serbian foreigners refused and so the Austrian-Hungarian foreigners declared war and the Russian foreigners/–

EUNUCH LIN: Who *used* to have an emperor/

PROFESSOR: Correct – also began to mobilise their army/

OLD SIX: Wait wait wait. So these Russian foreigners were the first to join in?

PROFESSOR: The Russian foreigners are friends with the Serbian foreig/ners.

EUNUCH LIN: They *don't* have an emperor/?

PROFESSOR: They're too small/ for an emperor.

OLD SIX: But now these Russian foreigners are not in this war because they're fighting against each other in their own country?

EUNUCH LIN: Because they want to get rid of their emperor like we did?

PROFESSOR: Correct.

BIG DOG: These foreigners are like a bad opera/

PROFESSOR: The German foreigners/

EUNUCH LIN: The evil German foreigners –

PROFESSOR: *(Wryly.)* The evil German foreigners/–

EUNUCH LIN: – who also have an emperor/

PROFESSOR: – and who are friends with the Austrian-Hungarian foreigners who don't like the Serbian foreigners, decide to declare war on the Russian foreigners/

OLD SIX: Not the Serbian foreigners?

PROFESSOR: They weren't interested in the Serbian foreigners/

EUNUCH LIN: Even though they don't like them?

BIG DOG bursts into a manic laughter that is obviously disguising great discomfort.

BIG DOG: Do you go round thinking about the pig shit you stepped in last week?

PROFESSOR: The French foreigners/–

EUNUCH LIN: Who are a republic/

OLD SIX: Like we are/ now.

EUNUCH LIN: So no emperor/

PROFESSOR: Correct – who are bound by treaty to the Russian foreigners, then find themselves at war with the German foreigners (and by extension, the Austrian-Hungarian foreigners) who then invade Belgium/

OLD SIX: Wait wait wait. What in the name of Buddha's tooth is Belgium?

BIG DOG: *(Muffled groan.)*

PROFESSOR: Belgium is a small nation between Germany and France.

EUNUCH LIN: Too small to have an emperor then?

PROFESSOR: Actually, no/

OLD SIX: These foreigners are a mighty bunch indeed!

BIG DOG: Mightier than you. You thought we were in Paris when we'd only reached Shanghai.

OLD SIX: The mechanical snake we travelled in took so long, how was I supposed to know we were still in China?

BIG DOG: The street signs were in Chinese!

EUNUCH LIN: And who's winning this mighty war, Professor?

PROFESSOR: It hangs in the balance. Our side waits for assistance from the mighty Americans/

EUNUCH LIN: The mighty Americans that banned us?

PROFESSOR: Under their Chinese Exclusion Act of 1882/

OLD SIX: Why did they ban us?

PROFESSOR: We work too hard.

EUNUCH LIN: Big Dog, they heard about you.

BIG DOG: *(Groans.)*

PROFESSOR: I must confess I have read as many newspapers and periodicals as I can lay hands on and at the end of it all I still have no heavenly idea why these foreigners are at war with each other.

EUNUCH LIN: At least we Chinese are not fighting anyone/

PROFESSOR: Except ourselves/–

BIG DOG: No shit/

PROFESSOR: – attempting to quell our own rebellions and civil strife like a land of fevered cannibals/

OLD SIX: Professor, these Westerners believe they are superior to we yellow people, do they not?

PROFESSOR: The Westerners believe all who are not of pale aspect to be inferior races.

OLD SIX: They don't think the Japanese are inferior though?

PROFESSOR: The Westerners certainly do believe the Japanese are inferior but the Japanese have purchased favour from the Westerners by supposedly using their powerful ships/–

EUNUCH LIN: Metal sea monsters/

PROFESSOR: – to protect everyone else's…metal sea monsters from the Germans' underwater…metal sea monsters/

BIG DOG: Underwater???

PROFESSOR: They can hide inside the sea and destroy other…metal sea monsters/

OLD SIX: They have sea monsters that can do this???

PROFESSOR: They already destroyed a ship killing over five hundred of our fellow Chinese labourers.

BIG DOG: Oh my sky/!

EUNUCH LIN: This was invented by the God of Chaos!

OLD SIX: Are there underwater sea monsters here, Professor?

PROFESSOR: In this ocean they reckon not. And they will shortly take us by rail across land.

EUNUCH LIN: So no underwater sea monsters/?

PROFESSOR: Not in Canada/

EUNUCH LIN: Thank the celestial stars!

OLD SIX: What's Canada?

PROFESSOR: A sovereign republic to the north of America.

EUNUCH LIN: So they don't have an emperor?

PROFESSOR: No, but they do have a punitive entry tax which is why we are to be caged up in wagons like smuggled farm stock.

EUNUCH LIN: Why?

PROFESSOR: Like their American neighbours they don't want us there.

BIG DOG: Does anyone under heaven not hate us Chinese?

EUNUCH LIN: *(Heavy irony.)* The Japanese like us.

OLD SIX: They certainly like our Shandong/

EUNUCH LIN: Their soldiers are everywhere!

OLD SIX: The Japanese have an emperor.

PROFESSOR: As well as imperial ambition. They eye our former Middle Kingdom like a ravening wolf does a piece of succulent meat.

EUNUCH LIN: I wish we still had an emperor.

BIG DOG: Not this again!

EUNUCH LIN: Nothing stopped. Nothing changed. Apart from our hairstyles.

And me.

PROFESSOR: Were you/–?

OLD SIX: Eunuch Lin's father thought his only future would be as a eunuch in the emperor's court.

BIG DOG: Then they did away with the emperor just as he was about to come of age.

EUNUCH LIN: He said I'd return home with the riches of the Great Qing and be celebrated far and wide. I was so young and I bled so much…and he sewed me up with a goose feather.

We hear the sound of a child as SECOND MOON travels in a circle around the men who appear to 'travel' as well but without changing position.

SECOND MOON: *(Singing.)*
'The moon is bright,
The wind is quiet,
The cradle moves so soft,
My little one now close your eyes,
Sleep, sleep, dreaming sweet dreams…'

EUNUCH LIN has given THE PROFESSOR a letter.

PROFESSOR: *(Reading.)* *'You will suffer the worst –'*

Where did you get this?

The lights fade to –

8. IN WHICH THE PROFESSOR READS
A LETTER FROM THE FOREIGNERS

– a train carriage (though there is no discernible difference in setting). OLD SIX and BIG DOG are asleep.

EUNUCH LIN: One of the German foreigners gave it to me on the way into the recruitment hall.

Go on, show me how to read it!

PROFESSOR: *(Reading.)* *'You will suffer the worst atrocities in the world and become spirits wandering on the field of battle…you will never find your way home and can never be buried in your native land.'*

EUNUCH LIN: …

Is that true?

PROFESSOR: It's propaganda.

EUNUCH LIN: What's that?

PROFESSOR: The foreigners think of us as a backward superstitious people/–

EUNUCH LIN: But is it true?

PROFESSOR: *(Continuing.)* – they seek to play on that superstition/

EUNUCH LIN: But is it true?

PROFESSOR: They're trying to scare/us –

EUNUCH LIN: But is it true???

PROFESSOR: …

From the other side of the world we hear SECOND MOON sing as THE PROFESSOR stares back at EUNUCH LIN…

SECOND MOON: *(Sings.)*
> *'The moon is bright, the wind is quiet,*
> *The tree leaves hang over the window,*
> *My little baby, sleep now soundly...'*

As we fade to –

9. A DRUNKEN RECKLESS MAN REFUSES TO BE REJECTED

SECOND MOON completes the circle to her house, where HEADMAN ZHANG waits for her. He is carrying a bottle and is clearly inebriated.

SECOND MOON: Headman Zhang! What wind blew you here?

HEADMAN ZHANG: I called here for you. You'd gone.

SECOND MOON: I walked.

HEADMAN ZHANG: So very far.

SECOND MOON: But a day's step.

HEADMAN ZHANG: You took the child?

SECOND MOON: The air did him good.

HEADMAN ZHANG: Daughter-in-law Moon, it hurts my heart you must endure this hardship.

He is close now. Too close.

SECOND MOON: It's...not good I be beholden to you/ Headman Zhang.

HEADMAN ZHANG: And why not?

SECOND MOON: My mother always taught me. On my own self and/ family only depend.

HEADMAN ZHANG: Your mother! We were close once. Did you know?

SECOND MOON: She never said.

HEADMAN ZHANG: A lady's honour,/ I understand.

SECOND MOON: She's not one to/ dwell on the past –

HEADMAN ZHANG: Chose your father instead. Left me with a sickly hag of a wife who couldn't even bear fruit before her lazy half-deck soul departed this/ world.

SECOND MOON: My mother thought highly of you/ I know that.

HEADMAN ZHANG: She died poor, didn't she? The horseshoer's three-eight-bitch of a wife/

SECOND MOON: Please…don't talk of my mother/ that way.

HEADMAN ZHANG: I loved your mother so very very much, Second Moon. Why wouldn't she love me back?

SECOND MOON: Maybe in the next life she'll ch/oose differently.

HEADMAN ZHANG smashes the bottle in rage.

HEADMAN ZHANG: I CARE NOT TWO PIECES OF TWIG FOR THE NEXT LIFE!

SECOND MOON screams as HEADMAN ZHANG grabs her and manhandles her onto the nearest available surface.

SECOND MOON: Please, Headman Zhang! I beg of you!

HEADMAN ZHANG: It's I who beg you, daughter. Hear me in this life, saviour of Mount Putuo/

He grabs her as she struggles to get away, roughly caressing her –

SECOND MOON: Please…I will sing for you clean for you wash for you but please! Not that/

HEADMAN ZHANG: *(At the same time.)* Hear my cries/
  oh pretty saviour…

SECOND MOON: Not that not that not that…NO!!!

  *– she breaks free, tries to run, he grabs her ankle and they both
  tumble into the pile of pots and pans and buckets, sending everything
  banging and clattering across the floor…*

  BANG BANG BANG!

  *A cacophony of noise as BIG DOG, OLD SIX, EUNUCH LIN, THE
  PROFESSOR plus countless others burst into the scene banging drums,
  shrilling pipes, shouting raucously in a spirit of wild celebration as
  we rapidly disperse into –*

10. THE HORSE SHOE VILLAGE VARIETY SHOW TROUPE PERFORMS HEROICS IN THEIR EUROPEAN DEBUT

*– a large open outdoor space which has become a 'performance area.'
BIG DOG, OLD SIX and EUNUCH LIN have even managed to recruit
THE PROFESSOR, who bangs a drum at the side.*

OLD SIX: *(Addressing the 'audience.')* Fellow workers of our
  newly-formed Chinese Labour Corps. My friends and
  myself are of meagre talent, but to celebrate our arrival in
  this magnificent and mighty land of France, we humbly
  beg to present for you just a small scene from our operatic
  version of the *Tale Of The Marsh.*

  Applause as we pick up their opera where we left it in Scene 2.

BIG DOG: *(As LANDLORD.)* *'Pilgrim friend! Already you are
  without your Miraculous Traveller. Your life is but a meal to that
  orange…stripy…animal.'*

OLD SIX: *(As PILGRIM WARRIOR, now tipsy.)*
  *'Trouble not your con-sci-ence, landlord friend.
  I'm a Qinghe County man!*

> *Full of fire and vim!*
> *Ha HOR Ha HOR!'*

The 'audience' cheer and laugh at PILGRIM WARRIOR's comic drunk bravery.

EUNUCH LIN: *(As LANDLORD'S WIFE.)*
> *'Eighteen bowls he has drunk*
> *His common sense all has sunk*
> *Out in the dark he dares to go*
> *His life is gone, oh woe is woe*
> *Husband stop him quick I entreat*
> *His handsome face is tiger's meat*
> *Let not the beast end his days*
> *Teach him Dao to learn the Way'*

BIG DOG: *(As LANDLORD.)* *'Silence, wife! Your rumination on this stranger's pretty face –'*

Cheers and whistles from the 'audience.'

'– has made me jealous. Let this cow's part, who eats and drinks far too much, go to his fate and the hell's minions take him!'

Raucous laughter.

Now PILGRIM WARRIOR is alone.

OLD SIX: *(As PILGRIM WARRIOR.)* *'Tiger?*
> *What tiger??*
> *HA!'*

A loud shrill burst of pipe and clash of cymbal and BIG DOG as TIGER explodes into the scene.

PILGRIM WARRIOR and TIGER 'pantomime' seeing each other.

BIG DOG: *(As TIGER.)* *'ROOOOOOOAAAAAAAAARRRRRR!!!'*

OLD SIX: *(As PILGRIM WARRIOR.)* *'AIYAAAARRRGGGGHHH!'*

BIG DOG: *(As TIGER.)* *'ROOOOAAAARRRROOORRRAARRR-OOOAAARR-OOAARR!!!!!!'*

TIGER accompanied by percussion and 'whoops' from EUNUCH LIN chases PILGRIM WARRIOR around the 'stage' to the cheers and laughter of the 'audience.' Suddenly OLD SIX turns.

OLD SIX: *(As PILGRIM WARRIOR.)* *'Be warned, oh tiger of the mountain. Wu Song The Pilgrim is a fearless Qinghe County man. Come near me and* I'll *eat* you *for dinner!'*

And now TIGER takes a charge at PILGRIM WARRIOR –

– back in Horse Shoe Village (but still in the discipline of 'opera') HEADMAN ZHANG takes a stylised lunge at SECOND MOON –

– while PILGRIM WARRIOR dodges, then pounds the TIGER's head again and again in a ludicrous display of stylised martial combat as the audience cheers loudly –

– as SECOND MOON swings a large metal pan at HEADMAN ZHANG's head –

– to an accompanying 'crash' from EUNUCH LIN's percussion.

HEADMAN ZHANG and TIGER are prostrate…

More raucous cheers and applause from the crowd who've watched the opera, while in the 'real world' SECOND MOON is far far away…

11. A WOMAN ALONE WITH A CORPSE AND A CRYING CHILD

SECOND MOON bends to examine HEADMAN ZHANG –

SECOND MOON: *(Realising he's dead.)* Oh no.

Oh no.

NOOOOOOO!!!!

She smashes the pan onto the floor. It clangs cacophonously. Grabs another pan, does the same. Grabs another pan. Again and again and again...

Something stops her.

The child is crying. She looks over.

Now there are deafening explosions. Does she hear them?

They're not 'here.' The explosions are...

12. IN WHICH A DANCING EUNUCH SINGS TO A SKY OF DESTRUCTION

...on the other side of the world, where BIG DOG, OLD SIX, EUNUCH LIN and THE PROFESSOR are cowering beneath an onslaught of large guns and bombs.

OLD SIX: I thought they said we'd be miles from the front line.

PROFESSOR: We are!

BOOM!

BIG DOG: If that was miles from the front line my third uncle is Buddha.

EUNUCH LIN: Don't be disrespectful/ now, Brother Dog.

BOOM!

PROFESSOR: The range of these foreigners' weapons is indeed testament to their profound industrial advancement/

BOOM!

BIG DOG: And now here we are, caught in the middle of their profound industrial advancement like idiot fucking turtle heads.

60

OLD SIX: My senses! I can't even feel my arms and legs anymore!

EUNUCH LIN: Never fear, brothers, never fear the German eggs.

EUNUCH LIN suddenly runs into the open –

OLD SIX: What the/ fuck?

BIG DOG: Get back! Get/ back!

PROFESSOR: Where are you/ going?

Now it is raining as explosions go off in the mid-distance.

EUNUCH LIN: I'm a magical opera star! I'm not afraid!

PROFESSOR: They'll kill you, Eunuch Lin, they'll kill/ you!

EUNUCH LIN: I bring love of all mankind!

BIG DOG: Get back here now, you fucking forgetter of the eight dummy-melon!

BOOM!

An explosion, near, but EUNUCH LIN, undeterred, begins to dance in the rain.

EUNUCH LIN: Ha ha ha! These German eggs may bang and burst but they aim them about as well as an old death-gripping man taking a piss first thing in the morning/

OLD SIX: They don't need to aim them. They can miss by a hundred *li* and still leave you scattered in so many pieces all the devils in hell won't be able to reassemble you for the afterlife.

EUNUCH LIN: Good! Good! Let them scatter small parts of a lonely eunuch boy who will never know love all across the fields of Europe. That I may fertilise these Western lands so these angry foreigners will no longer murder and conquer everything in their wide sight.

BIG DOG: You fucking mad little runt!

EUNUCH LIN: Let us declare peace on these red-lipped Western barbarians/

OLD SIX: What are you on about, you stupid plague god?

EUNUCH LIN: They declare their war. Let us celestial Chinese declare our peace.

He dances in the rain and sings:

'These strange things which barbarians have,
Have devil guts that make them go,
But we are happier people,
Who make no kin with the devil'

And now the bombing subsides as the sun begins to emerge from behind the clouds on a boy dancing in the rain.

BIG DOG: He made it stop! Eunuch Lin made it stop!

OLD SIX: The heavens have made him their mystic carrier of harmony!

EUNUCH LIN continues to sing.

EUNUCH LIN: *(Sings.)*
'For the devil is a man of fury and sound
Who lives in a big dark cave
Drag him out to the pure sunshine
And chase his evil away'

BIG DOG: Eunuch Lin! Eunuch Lin, you bounteous little death-scarer, you!

EUNUCH LIN: Join in, friends!

Sings on as the rest join him –

'For/ the devil is a man of fury and sound...'

As they sing, they fade momentarily into silhouette. Although we can hear them in the background we are now with SECOND MOON, carrying her child, who takes up the song...

SECOND MOON: *(Singing.)*
'The devil is a man of fury and sound...'

SECOND MOON looks around her, looks over at HEADMAN ZHANG's dead body, panic in her eyes, but keeps her voice as calm and soothing as possible –

'Who lives in a big dark cave...'

(To the child.) I have to go now. You can never see me.
Never know of me –

The child cries.

Hush now, my child. This life is like red dust on the wind.

With the child in her arms, SECOND MOON walks slowly...

SECOND MOON: *(Singing.)*
'Drag him out to the pure sunshine
And chase his evil away...'

She suddenly turns and runs...

...as the deafening sound of explosions decimate the world around her revealing –

– OLD SIX, BIG DOG, EUNUCH LIN and THE PROFESSOR dancing wildly in the rain.

EUNUCH LIN/OLD SIX/BIG DOG/PROFESSOR: *(Singing.)*
'For the devil is a cunt who grunts and farts
And fucks his mother's arse
He has the bladder of a pig instead of a heart
And his cock is made of brass'

Opera pipes, explosions…

Lights out.

END OF ACT ONE.

Act Two

1. WEDGE: THE 'CHINK CAMP'

In the darkness.

LABOURERS: *(Singing.)*
  'Thick mist now hides the sun
  Gentle pattering spots
  Urges the dull day on...'

  Now we see the stage has been transformed into the dwelling of the Chinese labourers behind the front line in France. A sign above reads 'Chink Camp,' where we see OLD SIX, BIG DOG, EUNUCH LIN and THE PROFESSOR, with others around them, working, carrying, digging...

LABOURERS: *(Singing.)*
  'Who says there is no grief in this world?
  Alas! Alas!
  In the rains the river is not controlled
  Alas! Alas!'

  Now we see a sign. A sign that says – 'ON NO ACCOUNT TALK TO THE CHINESE' with graffiti scrawled underneath – 'WHO CAN TALK TO CHINKS?'

  A bell rings – Ding-ding-ding!

  It has the same rhythm as a Chinese theatre 'clack-clack-clack.'

  The workers line up as if they are going to either work or perform.

  THE PROFESSOR stands slightly off, holding paper signs that we only see the back of.

OLD SIX: I am Old Six. In the drama I play all the heroes.

  We hear: clack-clack-clack.

OLD SIX performs a stylised Chinese theatre version of an English officer talking bad Mandarin: 'WO-YAO-BA-GE-REN-CHU-NA-HEN-KUAI!'

They all turn to look at THE PROFESSOR, who holds up a sign, which reads: 'I WANT EIGHT MEN TO GO OVER THERE VERY QUICKLY.'

EUNUCH LIN: I am Eunuch Lin. I play all the women in the drama.

We hear: clack-clack-clack!

EUNUCH LIN performs a stylised Chinese theatre version of an English officer talking bad Mandarin: 'ZHE-TANZI-LIBIAN-BU-SHI-HENG-GANJING!'

They look at THE PROFESSOR, who holds up another sign, which reads: 'THE INSIDE OF THIS TENT IS NOT VERY CLEAN.'

BIG DOG: I am Big Dog. In the drama I play clowns and animals.

We hear: clack-clack-clack!

BIG DOG performs a stylised Chinese theatre version of an English officer talking bad Mandarin: 'NI-YINGGAI-MINGTIAN-XIZAO!!!!!'

They look at THE PROFESSOR, who holds up another sign, which reads: 'YOU MUST HAVE A BATH TOMORROW.'

DING-DING-DING! Louder, more insistent.

PROFESSOR: Orders from Ganger Li, brothers. As the shelling's stopped an hour now, they want us out *(indicates the front) there* again.

Beat as the men absorb this.

EUNUCH LIN: *(Singing softly.)*
 'Broken trees upon the wasteland
 Tell of winter's chill...'

 As we transform into –

2. SHIFTING CORPSES AND A DISCOURSE ON CHINESE THEATRE BEFORE AN ENCOUNTER WITH THE 'ENEMY'

An explosion in the distance as we travel into a much darker, deadlier place. OLD SIX, THE PROFESSOR, BIG DOG and EUNUCH LIN huddle together as they descend into our version of 'The Underworld.'

EUNUCH LIN continues to sing.

EUNUCH LIN: *(Sings.)*
 '...God of nature, follow us safely
 Upon your mercy, still...'

 – as the light changes on himself, OLD SIX, BIG DOG and THE PROFESSOR in an otherwise deserted field of mud. They have spades and a wheelbarrow or cart, and are surrounded by mist.

BIG DOG: It stinks here.

OLD SIX: Stinks of death.

BIG DOG: I didn't reckon on this.

OLD SIX: This place is...

PROFESSOR: This place is necessity.

OLD SIX: This much destruction of life is necessity?

PROFESSOR: Warfare is fraught with necessity. Of necessity, someone has to dig trenches. Of necessity, someone has to clean their machines. Of necessity, someone has to clear away their dead/

OLD SIX: And allow their tortured lonely foreign ghosts who are still howling in pain and misery to pursue us wherever we go, covering us with their death and bad luck that seeps inside us like moss growing on a stone.

A distant explosion.

EUNUCH LIN: I thought they said it had stopped.

PROFESSOR: This is the big push. The German foreigners sense their final chance while our side waits for their mighty American brothers to join them.

BIG DOG: Brother Eunuch, keep singing. Chase those poor dead foreigners safely away into their big nose afterlife.

EUNUCH LIN: *(Sings.)*
'Could I convert stones to nod whose head's so high?
Or cut my flesh to patch up the skulls so nigh?
To help the dead ones wake up now I would like
Let all worldlings learn of death before they die!'

BIG DOG: *(At the same time.)* That fellow from the South told me. The French labour camp is different from ours. They work in the factories. With *women*. They're safe away from the battlefield. They can go out at night into the town and have a meal and a drink and walk and play.

And there are fox-spirit women there for sale.

EUNUCH LIN: *(Sings.)*
'Through sense comes all knowing
When you look with your eyes
Do not fail to see with your mind
Where deep waters are, all movement is so sluggish
The profound man speaks slow and with care'

PROFESSOR: *(At the same time.)* Liberty, equality, fraternity.

BIG DOG: Is that what it is?

PROFESSOR: The French foreigners like to give that impression.

BIG DOG: And our British don't?

PROFESSOR: 'Our' British foreigners wish to preserve the superiority of their culture.

BIG DOG: I want to go there.

OLD SIX: Where?

BIG DOG: The French camp.

OLD SIX: How are you are going to get there?

BIG DOG: Foreign barbarians can't tell one yellow shit stick from another. You think they give a fuck?

OLD SIX: They'll give a fuck about you wandering around Foreign Land like Monkey going West, you stupid pig's cock.

BIG DOG: They won't even know! In French Big Nose Camp they'll call a name. When there's no answer, I'll know some poor peasant's dead so I'll take his place and name/

OLD SIX: You'll take a dead man's place?

BIG DOG: We have to clear up their foreign dead, don't we? I've got so much bad fortune crawling all over me now, I might as well drink good wine and fuck some foreign fox-spirits in the miserable time I have left.

PROFESSOR: They do a roll-call. Every morning.

BIG DOG: Even in the land of liberty and equality?

PROFESSOR: The tripartite motto doesn't apply to Middle Kingdom/ workers –

BIG DOG: I don't want a motto I want a woman/

PROFESSOR: They'll search for you.

BIG DOG: Grandmother from your mother's side! They called out Lucky Cheek's name the other day and he wasn't there and they know he's gone and died somewhere and they don't care. They're fighting a war, not playing Hunt The Yellowman.

PROFESSOR: Brother Dog, your reasoning is not entirely without merit but, as the raw materiel in their foreign war machine, they may just wish to keep track/ of you.

BIG DOG: We're all the fucking same! Even to our own kind. Back in the Qing an uncle of mine got himself executed in someone's place so he could feed his starving family.

OLD SIX: Already we're in the middle numbers of the levels of hell and you wish to go further in?

PROFESSOR: Oh heaven!

There's one right there.

OLD SIX: Where?

PROFESSOR: There. Hidden down there in the mud.

BIG DOG: That's so horrible.

OLD SIX: Whose turn is it?

PROFESSOR: It's mine. I'll go.

OLD SIX: You did the last one.

PROFESSOR: I'm less superstitious than you.

BIG DOG: *(To THE PROFESSOR.)* You're like a phoenix in a briar patch.

PROFESSOR: I just happen to be able to read/

BIG DOG: That's what I meant.

PROFESSOR: Hold on to me. I should be able to drag him up.

OLD SIX: I've got you/

PROFESSOR: By the vision of the two generals but he's heavy!

EUNUCH LIN: His light spirit is flying in the air leaving his corpse weighed like lead.

BIG DOG: I've got you as well/

PROFESSOR: He's stuck in the mud.

EUNUCH LIN: Fear not, oh wise Professor, we'll perform your favourite opera part this evening.

PROFESSOR: I don't have a favourite opera part.

EUNUCH LIN: But you know operas?

OLD SIX: Pull him the other way/

BIG DOG: Learned man like/ you.

OLD SIX: That way the mud might release/ him.

PROFESSOR: I know operas.

BIG DOG: Maybe he just doesn't want to hear *us* do them.

PROFESSOR: I don't want to hear Zhongduxui herself do them. Heave!

OLD SIX: Heave!

BIG DOG: Heave!

EUNUCH LIN: Professor! Pro/fessor!

PROFESSOR: I can't hold/him!

OLD SIX: NO!

BIG DOG: Steady, Old Six!

PROFESSOR: Aaargh!

OLD SIX: GET HIM OFF ME! GET HIM OFF ME!

BIG DOG: There. There/

OLD SIX: GET HIM OFF!!!

BIG DOG: I've got it!

OLD SIX: AAAAAARRRRRGHHHH!!!

EUNUCH LIN: Get him in the barrow.

OLD SIX: FUCK!

BIG DOG: There.

OLD SIX: FUUUUUUCCCCKKKK!!!!

FUUUUUUCCCCKKKKKKK!!!!

BIG DOG: Sing to him, Eunuch Lin. Appease his angry spirit.

EUNUCH LIN: At least he died somewhere near his own land.
Maybe his spirit can find its way home.

*THE PROFESSOR is laughing. A long, slightly hysterical sound, that
stops them all in their tracks...*

PROFESSOR: You ask me why I have no wish to hear you
perform opera. I hate our redundant asinine Chinese
theatre like I hate our superstitious fish-wife culture which
is inside me like the blood in my veins.

In Europe they have dramas that blow apart their society
and pull it back together again in a different shape.

People blame the foreigners for our weakness. I don't
blame the foreigners. It's *us*. It's our drunk on sack wine
passive Confucian horse manure that renders us devoid
of *thought*.

You cling to your happy nature to keep the bad spirits away all you damn well like. I want something *REAL*! Something/ *REAL*!

SUDDENLY: a GERMAN SOLDIER has emerged from the mist. He is in full uniform, helmet and gas mask, so his face is invisible. To our Chinese labourers he is a terrifying vision. But the German is equally nonplussed by the sight of four Chinese workers in the middle of a European battlefield.

Now, he does raise his rifle but BIG DOG has had time to react and –

CRASH!

– BIG DOG whacks the GERMAN SOLDIER hard around the head with his spade, sending him spinning, disorientated –

CRASH!

BIG DOG whacks the GERMAN SOLDIER again – CRASH! CRASH! CRASH!

They all join in, hitting the GERMAN SOLDIER with spades, kicking, punching, until the soldier lies dead at their feet, but OLD SIX continues hitting the corpse again and again until BIG DOG drags him off –

BIG DOG: Enough, Brother Six/

OLD SIX: His blood's all over me! His brains are all over me! Let me see! Let me see this foreign pig's face/

BIG DOG: Brother Six,/ no –

OLD SIX: Let me see!

He tears open the gas mask. SECOND MOON's face stares back at him.

OLD SIX: NO! NO! NO!

He silently weeps.

EUNUCH LIN: You bashed his head in!

BIG DOG: Real enough for you, Professor?

EUNUCH LIN: You bashed his head in!

Shaken, they leave, as the 'corpse' becomes SECOND MOON, who slowly rises and performs her 'story' –

SECOND MOON: *(Opera style.)*
'On-the-stage: I was a miraculous traveller
In-the-world: I was treated with spite like wolf's bane
Cast-out-denied: by my own husband's family
In the yellow springs of hell, there's no worse criminal there:
I-I-I'm a woman who killed a powerful man
Now rain on the Xiao-Xiang pours on down
"These-these-these clouds that can hide the sky"
"This wind that will wrench out rocks"
"These sheets like knives that will run me through"
But on-on-on!
Magic talismans that will run eight hundred li *a day*
Miraculous Traveller, on!
My life is the opera'

SECOND MOON 'travels' opera-style as we hear the low chuckle of a character we haven't met previously…

3. EUNUCH LIN PLAYS 'FAN-TAN' WITH A MAN FROM THE HUAI PLAIN AND THE OPERA TROUPE MEETS ITS END

WILD SWAN: Well, if we're doing 'variety show'…

He performs 'opera style'.

'The name I'm called is Wild Swan
The Huai River plain is where I'm from
Where the wind blows in from the land of Mongols
The river there fills with dust and silt
Nothing grows and the floods there rumble

As your eyes and nose choke on Heaven's guilt
Because you can't farm a living so if you can you'll rob'

I'm saying this because I don't want these scabby donkey actors from Shandong making me a villain in their milkweed play. Actors! You can't trust them. I fucking hate actors!

– now we are back in the 'Chink Camp' in France. With the sign saying 'Chink Camp'. With the warning that no white officers are to talk to any Chinese. OLD SIX, BIG DOG, EUNUCH LIN and THE PROFESSOR are gathered around.

Well, friends? Do I pass the test? Can I be an 'actor'?

Set up the game, book fool!

PROFESSOR: The Huai River needs to flow with more patience.

THE PROFESSOR is hurriedly preparing a rough makeshift table for a 'fan-tan' game with lids and buttons.

WILD SWAN: The Huai River will piss in your face. Did all your books teach you how to dive for poisonous dragons, friend?

Mimes cunnilingus action. Bursts into laughter. There is an uneasy air amongst the rest.

EUNUCH LIN: Oh wild Wild Swan, are you not afeared to take on the Shandong eunuch god of gambling?

WILD SWAN: If there's one thing I hate even more than an actor it's a eunuch.

EUNUCH LIN: Been defeated by eunuchs before then, Wild Swan?

WILD SWAN: The entire Ming Dynasty was defeated by you treacherous cut-sleeve crabs. And the Han. And the house of Wu. And the Qin. All brought down by demon-seed smooth-crotches. *(To THE PROFESSOR.)* Enough history for you, phoenix-flatterer?

EUNUCH LIN: You speak of power, oh Swan. To the rest of us, the world's affairs rush on like an endless stream.

BIG DOG: Don't play with him, Eunuch Lin. He has the look of a vinegar loser about him.

WILD SWAN: *(To BIG DOG.)* Forgetters of the eight forget their sense of humour as well now it seems. That's no use if you want to mount the dragon to be proper entertainers.

BIG DOG: Your tongue is as rude as the Huai River/ itself, friend.

OLD SIX: Peace, Big Dog, this one knows nothing but trouble.

WILD SWAN: And you look like a regular low three-down-four/ piss-face.

PROFESSOR: Harmony, friends, and good will/

WILD SWAN: *(To OLD SIX, indicating THE PROFESSOR.)* Still harping on that wife of yours back in Shandong, donkey boy? Begging this book-face half-melon to write fish-letters to her. She's long gone, friend. Like Elder Brother Wu's wife in your shitty play/

OLD SIX: *(Going to rise.)* I'll forget my/self in a minute –

BIG DOG: *(Restraining him.)* Mildly, Brother Six/

WILD SWAN: She'll be fanning your grave before you're even in it. Everyone knows the hearts of women are like turning wheels. You think she gives a fuck who combs her hair as long as the sassy villain has money?

EUNUCH LIN: *(Topping them all.)* SHALL WE PLAY FAN-TAN THEN????

Silence.

OLD SIX: *(Decisively.)* Why not? Play him, brother Eunuch.

BIG DOG: This is tweaking the/ tiger's whiskers –

WILD SWAN: *(Referring to EUNUCH LIN.)* Lady-lady gate here likes to gamble then?

EUNUCH LIN: *(To WILD SWAN.)* As much as your mother likes turtle heads, oh fiery Swan.

WILD SWAN roars with laughter.

WILD SWAN: *(Laughing.)* I fuck!

BIG DOG drags OLD SIX to one side –

BIG DOG: We should tell this evil stick to go.

OLD SIX: Be not fearful, Brother Dog, our songbird eunuch never loses.

BIG DOG: That fellow has a look of death about him.

OLD SIX: *(Suddenly snapping.)* No! It's I, I who have the look of death about me!

EUNUCH LIN: Old Six, play fan-tan with us!

OLD SIX: Even now, my soul is in the mountain of knives/

WILD SWAN: Witness me defeat this blow-server and return with his money back to the fox-bitches of the flood land.

EUNUCH LIN: *(Laughing.)* The only thing you'll be returning with is your hurt face, oh wild one.

OLD SIX has shrugged off BIG DOG and now sits at the fan-tan table.

OLD SIX: Deal, Professor!

PROFESSOR: (–)

OLD SIX: Deal, Professor. I will enjoy watching this half-empty bottle of vinegar lose to a magical opera eunuch.

BIG DOG shrugs.

THE PROFESSOR begins to deal. They play. Time passes.

Then –

PROFESSOR: He wins again! The eunuch wins again!

WILD SWAN: Pig's bladder fairy boy, you've surely bribed the fates/

BIG DOG: *(Enjoying this in spite of himself.)* The deities like his dancing, Wild/ Swan.

WILD SWAN: Deal, book face. I need to beat this glass fairy once and for all.

OLD SIX: I told you, Brother Swan, this is our magical eunuch. No harm will befall us while The Great Lin carries his song.

WILD SWAN: He's as magical as your mother's back door, you surly oaf.

OLD SIX: Fuck your second uncle, Wild Swan, you're never beating the fabled gambler from Shandong province.

BIG DOG: Even the fiercest warriors of the marsh knew when to retreat, Wild Swan.

OLD SIX: You're playing with the Kongming of fan-tan, oh salty one.

WILD SWAN: *(To THE PROFESSOR.)* Lift that fucking lid, Professor Shitface, or I'll make you wear it like a helmet.

THE PROFESSOR lifts the improvised metal lid to reveal a small heap of buttons.

EUNUCH LIN: *(In celebration.)* Again!

WILD SWAN: You fucking cheated me, you glass fairy traitor.

EUNUCH LIN: What did you say, brother?

WILD SWAN: You cheated me. You, you're in league with this *(indicates THE PROFESSOR)* intellectual skin-bag of treacherous bones and the two of you devious gamble-sticks cheated me.

PROFESSOR: Brother Swan, you saw the game for yourself, there was no pathway/ for cheating.

WILD SWAN: Who knows what tricks you Shandong pig-lovers have from this chrysanthemum-arsed fairy whoring himself out to the god of stratagem?

OLD SIX: Eat vinegar, oh bitter swan.

EUNUCH LIN: Shall I compose an aria of loss for you, wild one?

EUNUCH LIN rises and starts to sing –

'Awaken to emptiness
Awaken beyond
On the river of bitterness
Floats an angry wild swan'

WILD SWAN: Fuck all your uncles and cousins and rape your mother with broken glass, you little swine/

Suddenly WILD SWAN rises, toppling the table and swinging his arm, as EUNUCH LIN reels back as if blown by a 'swoosh' –

Now there is blood. Then the realisation that WILD SWAN is holding some form of blade.

Blood pours from EUNUCH LIN's jugular…Shocked, stunned silence…

EUNUCH LIN looks imploringly at BIG DOG and OLD SIX. Attempts to go to them –

Staggers and collapses.

ALL: Eunuch Lin/Little Brother/Brother Eunuch… *(Etc.)*

EUNUCH LIN gasps and chokes as his life ebbs away.

OLD SIX: How?

How????

WILD SWAN chuckles. A low, terrible sound.

WILD SWAN: I've killed one of you pig lovers with my blade of autumn streams. You think I can't kill you all?

Come on then! Come on then, you Shandong inbreds! I'll chew your flesh!

BANG BANG BANG!

WILD SWAN, hit by a hail of bullets, staggers – BANG BANG BANG!

More bullets and now WILD SWAN drops to the floor, dead.

Now a voice over a megaphone. Clipped, English –

ENGLISH OFFICER: *(Off.)* Listen up, Chinese Labour Corps. There is to be no gambling or fighting in the Chinese Camp. This is the British Army and there will be discipline. Any Chinese caught gambling will be charged and punished. Any Chinese seen fighting or brandishing a weapon is liable to be shot on sight. Now, bury your dead and get to sleep. At the double!

It is as if the Chinese labourers have been listening in a trance to the foreign overlord. Now, they snap out of it and all run to where EUNUCH LIN is breathing his last –

BIG DOG: Brother Eunuch! Brother Eunuch!

OLD SIX: Can't we stop his bleeding, Pro/fessor?

PROFESSOR: I can't.

OLD SIX: But you know everything, Professor. You've read
every book there is you know everything there is to know
about our world and our history surely surely surely you
can make our brother better ag/ain –

PROFESSOR: He's lost too much already.

*BIG DOG holds EUNUCH LIN in his arms with infinite tenderness
as the terrified boy looks up at him, gasping, gurgling and spluttering
desperately, clinging to life with everything he has –*

BIG DOG: *(Sings softly.)*
'Dark is the night and gone is the day
Magic Traveller, show the Way…'

EUNUCH LIN: *(One last effort.)* Fear not, Brother…Big Dog…
I'm a magical –

EUNUCH LIN has gone. Silence.

BIG DOG: *(Low moaning turning to helpless tears.)* Aiiiii…aiiii…
aiiii…aiiii

OLD SIX: What did I do what did I do what did I do…

From somewhere else we hear –

FRENCH OFFICER: *(Off.)* Quatre Huit Trois Cinq Trois!

OLD SIX: What did I…

The 'Chink Camp' sign is turned around so it reads –

4. BIG DOG DEFECTS TO THE MORE CORDIAL SIDE OF *ENTENTE CORDIALE*

– *'Le Camp Chinois.' BIG DOG, trying hard to look inconspicuous, falls in with the rest of the men. One or two of them look at him but no one takes much notice.*

FRENCH OFFICER: *(Off.)* Quatre Huit Trois Cinq Quatre!

A man near BIG DOG raises his hand.

FRENCH OFFICER: *(Off.)* Quatre Huit Trois Cinq Cinq!

Another man near BIG DOG raises his hand.

FRENCH OFFICER: *(Off.)* Quatre Huit Trois Cinq Six!

No one moves.

FRENCH OFFICER: *(Off.)* Quatre Huit Trois Cinq Six!

Still no one moves.

Quatre Huit Trois Cinq Six???

BIG DOG thrusts up his hand. One man near him looks askance, but BIG DOG flashes him a 'warning' look and the man looks away again.

FRENCH OFFICER: *(Off, in French.)* Were you sleeping there, 48356? When I call your name, respond! This goes for all of you. If you don't, I mark you as dead and I know how suspicious you Chinese are about that, eh? Do you understand?

BIG DOG, who knows even less French than he does English, responds to the silence the only way he knows how: by nodding vigorously and attempting a kind of salute. A couple of men near him laugh.

FRENCH OFFICER: *(Off, in French.)* Not bad, you. Very good. I could make a soldier of you, maybe. Now, all of you, get to work!

The Chinese begin to march off to work. BIG DOG falls in easily with the rest…

5. IN WHICH A LETTER IS DICTATED AND A MIRACULOUS TRAVELLER ENCOUNTERS A FOLLOWER OF CHRIST

…the scene is broken by OLD SIX suddenly walking at speed in a circle around the whole stage 'opera style' as THE PROFESSOR trails after him in the 'real world' carrying a pen and paper.

PROFESSOR: What should I write, Brother Six?

What should I write?

To your wife Second Moon?

The word 'wife' stops OLD SIX in his tracks for a second.

OLD SIX: Just…

As THE PROFESSOR prepares to take dictation and OLD SIX thinks, SECOND MOON suddenly appears, travelling the same circle in a slow motion 'opera walk' that indicates graceful swift movement. She wears her 'opera' coat but otherwise appears bedraggled.

OLD SIX doesn't 'see' SECOND MOON but seems to sense her presence, moving after her in the circle –

OLD SIX: To my wife and child…

PROFESSOR: *(Writing.)* To my wife and child…

OLD SIX: Life goes well here in the fields of F–

ENGLISH OFFICER: *(Off, cutting in. OLD SIX and THE PROFESSOR immediately stop.)* Redact! No details of geographic location shall be divulged in any correspondence lest such correspondence fall into enemy hands rendering vital intelligence information to the enemy.

OLD SIX and THE PROFESSOR commence moving again –

OLD SIX: I spend my days at toil with a spade as I dig mighty tr–

ENGLISH OFFICER: *(Off, cutting in. OLD SIX and THE PROFESSOR immediately stop.)* Redact! No details of duties performed shall be divulged lest correspondence fall into enemy hands thus rendering vital intelligence to the enemy of our military activities.

OLD SIX and THE PROFESSOR commence moving again. As they do another figure in a dapper Western suit joins SECOND MOON's circle –

OLD SIX: We and our fellow Middle Land workers –

ENGLISH OFFICER: *(Off, cutting in.)* Redact! No information of coloured labourer activity whatsoever shall be divulged –

The ENGLISH OFFICER is interrupted by SECOND MOON on the other side of the world –

SECOND MOON: *(To the FOLLOWER OF CHRIST.)* GET BACK!!!

FOLLOWER OF CHRIST: I mean you no harm, miss. I can assure you/

OLD SIX: *(Still dictating but standing still.)* Eunuch Lin and Big Dog…

PROFESSOR: *(But he doesn't write.)* Eunuch Lin and Big Dog –

They are interrupted by SECOND MOON who advances threateningly towards THE FOLLOWER OF CHRIST who backs away in a circle around OLD SIX and THE PROFESSOR –

SECOND MOON: Don't think I can't kill you. I may have killed before.

FOLLOWER OF CHRIST: It's not my business what you have done in your past.

SECOND MOON: It's not your business what I do now.

OLD SIX: *(Attempting to be cheerful.)* Eunuch Lin and Big Dog are well and healthy –

SECOND MOON: Who are you?

FOLLOWER OF CHRIST: I'm a follower of Christ.

OLD SIX: *(Still dictating but standing still.)* Eunuch Lin teaches me opera circles –

SECOND MOON: Was your Lord Christ a Miraculous Traveller?

FOLLOWER OF CHRIST: He walked the Way of Sorrows. He was crucified on the cross with a crown of thorns –

OLD SIX: *(Still dictating but standing still.)* – and Big Dog enjoys the sight of poppy flowers –

ENGLISH OFFICER: *(Off, cutting in.)* Redact!

SECOND MOON laughs –

SECOND MOON: What kind of straw head gets himself nailed to a wooden cross?

ENGLISH OFFICER: *(Off, cutting in.)* No information of foliage or topography particular to local/geography shall be divulged lest correspondence fall into enemy hands thus rendering vital intelligence to the enemy –

FOLLOWER OF CHRIST: *(At the same time.)* He died for our sins/

SECOND MOON: *(At the same time.)* Even mine?

FOLLOWER OF CHRIST: *(At the same time.)* All of mankind/

SECOND MOON: But I murdered *man*kind!

OLD SIX: *(Dictating.)* But Eunuch Lin and Big Dog are well and healthy/

PROFESSOR: Are you sure you shouldn't –?

SECOND MOON: *(Moving in a circle, narrating 'opera style':)*
'I-I-I killed the Headman who would force himself on me
The mighty village Headman who would sate his pleas'

OLD SIX: *(Continuing determinedly.)* If you and Red Sky Child have need Headman Zhang will provide –

SECOND MOON: *(Continued.)*
'Now I-I-I'm the leak-brain fox-fiend who tempted a man
Left my child with a brother-in-law who cast me down from the clan'

OLD SIX: *(Aching sadness.)* May health and fortune bless your days/…

FOLLOWER OF CHRIST: Where will you go now?

OLD SIX: Your clumsy husband and father/…

FOLLOWER OF CHRIST: Miss…where will you go?

PROFESSOR: Do you want to sign it?

FOLLOWER OF CHRIST: Miss –

PROFESSOR: The way I taught you/–

SECOND MOON: France!

PROFESSOR: – from the thousand character simplified writing system the followers of Christ invented/

FOLLOWER OF CHRIST: You can't just go to France! There's vast…oceans, you can't/!

OLD SIX: That was the simplified version/?

SECOND MOON: But I can, Follower of Christ.

I'm the Miraculous Traveller. I can go anywhere and sing any song and tell any story.

And if I carry a story inside me how can an ocean stop me?

OLD SIX and SECOND MOON head in opposing circles just past each other as she and THE FOLLOWER OF CHRIST disappear, while OLD SIX takes a brush with red paint and clumsily (but swiftly) scrawls a pair of Chinese characters on the wall at the back...

6. IN WHICH OLD SIX ATTEMPTS TO LEARN TO TRAVEL

OLD SIX and THE PROFESSOR in the 'Chink Camp.'

PROFESSOR: How did you persuade the followers of Christ to teach you that?

OLD SIX: Told them I was writing a play.

PROFESSOR: It says 'killer'.

OLD SIX: It's my name.

PROFESSOR: Your name is Old Six.

OLD SIX: There were no jade circle steps or mandarin duck kicks but, just as Wu Song The Pilgrim murdered his brother's wife, so Old Six killed the eunuch/

PROFESSOR: You have to/ stop this –

OLD SIX: Big Dog thought so/

PROFESSOR: Big Dog grieved for Eunuch Lin's death, as/ did we all –

OLD SIX: What will the foreigners do with our poor Eunuch Lin in their afterlife? Make him work for them there/ as well –?

PROFESSOR: I believe there is no after/ life –

OLD SIX: They had no use for his opera song. It was just an ugly cacophonous screeching chaos to them –

PROFESSOR: *(Continuing, at the same time.)* – so it is no matter –

OLD SIX now begins to circle the stage, slowly at first, then faster and faster

OLD SIX: Hush now, Professor/

PROFESSOR: What/ are you…?

OLD SIX: I have to keep a perfect circle/

PROFESSOR: In the name of the deities, why?

OLD SIX: Because that's how we travel in an opera and I have to get to the end of the story!

PROFESSOR: Oh my sky!!!

OLD SIX paces the circle, faster and faster, manically –

OLD SIX: A circle, always a circle. Eunuch Lin/and Second Moon would practice the circle over and over again. Always a circle in the opera. No ugly straight lines and sharp corners in the opera. Everything's smooth and circular in the opera, nothing cuts nothing nothing nothing cuts –

PROFESSOR: *(At the same time.)* Listen to me. He could've died in this place or he could've died at home. There is no afterlife or yellow springs of hell or Auntie Meng tea or King Yama or road to rebirth. There is only here and

there is only now and when we're not here we
don't exist/–

OLD SIX: YOU'RE DISTURBING MY
CONCENTRATION!!!

THE PROFESSOR puts his hand over OLD SIX's mouth –

PROFESSOR: Shh! I don't want the rest to report you to the
big noses. I don't know what they'd do with you. Please!

OLD SIX: (–)(–)(–)

THE PROFESSOR takes his hand from OLD SIX's mouth.

OLD SIX: *(Quietly.)* My circle's wrong, Professor. I have to
learn. Because there's no one else now. I left my wife, Big
Dog left me and I killed the eunuch.

PROFESSOR: You didn't kill him/

OLD SIX: Killed him with my lone/liness.

PROFESSOR: Wild Swan/ killed Eunuch Lin.

OLD SIX: Killed him with my fear/

PROFESSOR: Life and death come to/ all of us –

OLD SIX: Killed him with my rage.

There'll be no one to tell our story.

We'll be gone from this world of dust and its boundless
bitter sea faster than the wings of a bird...

I have to tell our story.

PROFESSOR: Yes.

Yes.

You must .

But first. Please.

OLD SIX: (?)

PROFESSOR: You can speak the southern Shandong dialect?

OLD SIX: …

PROFESSOR: *(Producing a letter.)* Being able to read was such a gift. Now I read all the letters that come into our camp. Like Guanyin. Who hears all the world's sorrows.

Could you tell that fellow with the limp that his wife and children have all perished from starvation due to the bad crop this year?

OLD SIX looks at THE PROFESSOR. Nods slowly. Leaves.

THE PROFESSOR sits with his head in his hands as we hear the sounds of a song 'Plaisir D'Amour' in the background as if from miles away…

7. A SINGING LADY IN A BOX AND THE SHARING OF STORIES IN DIFFERENT LANGUAGES

…It comes from a gramophone player being carefully carried by a girl called MARIE. She wears a head scarf that conceals her face apart from her eyes. We are in some sort of 'common area' in a factory as the lights on THE PROFESSOR slowly dim. BIG DOG follows MARIE as she carefully places the gramophone player on the ground in front of them where they are both entranced by it.

Unbeknownst to himself BIG DOG's face is bright yellow.

MARIE speaks in French throughout.

BIG DOG: *(Mesmerised.)* I rode in a sea monster. Then saw the biggest guns ever that can destroy whole towns from twenty *li* away. Wooden machines that fly in the air and can rain down fire on us useless insects on the earth below. Metal boxes with caterpillar feet that spit death on everything in their path.

But now you show me a singing woman in a box…

To MARIE pointing at the gramophone –

That. Is the cow's cunt.

MARIE: *(French.)* Yes, it's good of them/

BIG DOG: It is. The cow's cunt!

MARIE: *(French.)* – to let us have music at all in the fac/tory…

BIG DOG: They didn't have singing women in boxes in our British big nose camp.

MARIE: *(French.)* It's their progressive way to motivate/ the workers –

BIG DOG: We didn't work with girls either –

MARIE: *(French.)* So our depression won't undermine their great war/ effort –

BIG DOG: I like this… *(it's a new word)* factory!

MARIE: *(French.)* – keep them cheerful and productive by playing them a song.

BIG DOG: Why do you wear this –

Pointing at MARIE's face scarf and miming it –

– on your face? Why?

MARIE: *(French, miming as she speaks.)* So my face doesn't turn bright yellow like yours, you stupid cheese sandwich.

BIG DOG: (?)

MARIE: *(French, producing a mirror.)* Here, I'll show you, potato man –

BIG DOG sees himself in the mirror.

BIG DOG: Shit on your second uncle's grave!

MARIE bursts into fits of giggles as BIG DOG attempts to rub the yellow off his face.

MARIE: *(French.)* As a child, was your cradle rocked too close to the wall?

BIG DOG: What is it? What is it?

MARIE: *(French, miming as she speaks.)* The munitions, stupid. The chemicals that go in the bombs, they make you go yellow. It's funny. They call you Chinamen 'yellow' but you're not. Not really. You are now though!

BIG DOG: *(Miming as he speaks.)* This. *(Points to his face.)* It lasts forever?

MARIE: *(French, suddenly serious.)* Yes.

It's permanent. I'm sorry

Pause.

No, you silly whore, it comes off!

She laughs again. Beat.

BIG DOG: *My* name – *(Points to himself.)* Well, it's not my name but everyone calls me it –

Points to himself again –

Big Dog.

Tries to mime and points to himself –

Big…

'Dog' action –

Woof!

MARIE: *(French.)* You…are a…fat dog…?

BIG DOG: Yes! Yes!

MARIE: *(French.)* This is your name???

BIG DOG: What's yours?

MARIE: *(French, pointing to herself.)* Marie.

BIG DOG: Are you sick?

MARIE: *(French.)* My name is Marie.

BIG DOG: I probably smell like a pig's mother's arse, excuse/
me.

MARIE: *(French.)* I am called…Marie.

BIG DOG: Very…poetic.

MARIE: *(French.)* I think we'd better stick to the music –

She starts to wind up the gramophone player again.

BIG DOG: Yes! Yes! Make the woman in the magic box sing
again.

'Plaisir D'Amour' plays again…

Ma-hi.

MARIE: *(French.)* Yes?

BIG DOG: *(Indicates the song.)* It's nice.

Tries to mime 'nice song' –

MARIE: *(French.)* I'm glad you like it.

BIG DOG: Did they only teach her one song before they put
her in the box?

MARIE: *(French.)* The words in the song are very beautiful…

She speaks the words as they play on the gramophone –

'The pleasure of love lasts only a moment,
The grief of love lasts a lifetime'

Of all places, of all names. Champagne. He choked on gas then lay drowning in a bombshell as the rats ate his stomach away...

BIG DOG: You're talking about sad things. I can tell.

MARIE: *(French.)* Ironic.

BIG DOG: My friend used to like to call us the 'magical Chinese'. He loved the theatre with all his soul but we both knew our plays were heavy and dull.

MARIE: *(French.)* This is nice. I talk. You talk. We don't understand a word each other's saying but the world turns and this absurd war feels a million miles away. For a moment.

BIG DOG: *(As if inspired.)* Or maybe our plays were just heavy and dull because they let me be in them. Because I was their friend.

MARIE: *(French.)* Come here. Let's dance.

BIG DOG: What are you –?

MARIE: *(French.)* I can teach you, Monsieur Dog. It's easy.

BIG DOG: Oh my sky!

MARIE: *(French.)* I've never danced with a foreigner before. Especially not one with a face like a canary's arse.

BIG DOG: You're laughing at my face again. I can tell.

They dance awkwardly but tenderly. It's a golden moment but already the world is encroaching back in...

'Plaisir d'amour ne dure qu'un moment
chagrin d'amour dure toute la vie…'

…as we fade back to THE PROFESSOR in the 'Chink Camp' as BIG DOG and MARIE dance in silhouette…

Enter OLD SIX.

THE PROFESSOR looks at OLD SIX…

OLD SIX nods.

THE PROFESSOR nods back. A bell rings sharply.

Then we hear –

ENGLISH OFFICER: *(Megaphone, off.)* Now listen up, Chinese Labour Corps. Last night one of your number hung themselves in the officers dugout. If any more of you must hang yourselves then be so good as to do it in your own dugouts. We don't like such a mess in ours. Now I need Chinese workers to clear this corpse. Now!

As before OLD SIX and THE PROFESSOR have listened as if in a trance.

OLD SIX: Help me, Professor.

THE PROFESSOR nods. They start to move off then –

PROFESSOR: One question: why did you choose the marsh tale for your play?

OLD SIX: Because they're a heroic warrior fraternity who do right by the poor.

PROFESSOR: And does it end well for them?

Now the French song again but the gramophone is winding down –

'Plaisir d'amour ne dure qu'un moment
chagrin d'amour dure toute la vie…'

As if sensing the imminent ending BIG DOG suddenly steps back –

BIG DOG: Can I live inside the magic box and sing to you when you're sad?

– but it isn't to be as OLD SIX and THE PROFESSOR gently move BIG DOG away and begin tying him to a pole as MARIE vanishes…

BIG DOG stares after but she is gone. We hear –

ENGLISH VOICE ON CRACKLY RADIO: Hostilities to cease. This morning, eleven hours. On the eleventh day of the eleventh month. The year of our lord, 1918.

Hostilities cease…

…as THE PROFESSOR and OLD SIX tie BIG DOG to the pole…

8. BIG DOG RETURNS

Early morning. A sense of calm.

PROFESSOR: My apologies, Brother Big Dog. Ganger Li insisted because the English officers instructed him they need an example set.

BIG DOG: It's nothing they wouldn't do to their own foreign big-nose soldiers. It's almost an honour.

PROFESSOR: The honour will be over soon.

BIG DOG: Why?

PROFESSOR: The war is ending. They said.

BIG DOG: Who won?

PROFESSOR: The fatigued Germans have finally collapsed from exhaustion. They had no workers from far-off lands to dig their trenches and mend their tanks.

BIG DOG: Roll your mother's egg!

PROFESSOR: They'll keep us long enough to clear their battlefield. Make it nice and neat for them. Now they're finished with it for the time being.

BIG DOG: Do you think they'll come and flood our land with opium again now they have nothing to occupy them once more?

PROFESSOR: Our brave new republic will never be that enfeebled again, Big Dog. Thanks to us. They're convening the peace conference already. And we have a place there!

BIG DOG: A place at the table of fire-wielding foreigners!

PROFESSOR: Two places perhaps. It appears we now have a government in the South as well.

BIG DOG: The foreigners will be impressed by our mighty two-headed dragon.

PROFESSOR: Providing we don't eat ourselves.

BIG DOG: But at least these victorious Westerners now have to consider our claims?

PROFESSOR: The Shandong territories *will* return to us.

And we played our part.

BIG DOG: *(Indicating OLD SIX who has entered during the above.)* He was right.

About this. About everything.

Now OLD SIX moves forward. Silence.

BIG DOG and OLD SIX look at each other. Silence as they both struggle for the words. Then –

OLD SIX: What happened to your face?

BIG DOG: *Cul de canari.*

OLD SIX: What's that?

BIG DOG: Something to do with the magic these foreigners use in their smelly egg bombs. I thought it would make good opera make-up.

OLD SIX: …

    It was my fault/

BIG DOG: No/

OLD SIX: I taunted the wild swan.

BIG DOG: It wasn't you.

OLD SIX: I wanted the swan to lose/face

BIG DOG: I did too. It was both of us.

OLD SIX: *(To THE PROFESSOR.)* Will the foreigners allow us to take Eunuch Lin home?

PROFESSOR: I'm sure they never will.

OLD SIX: Then our song stays here.

    The silence swells into firecrackers in the distance, the sound of 'armistice': music, celebration, announcements in all European languages, louder and louder as BIG DOG is released from his bonds as the sounds of celebration turn into –

9. THE GATE OF GHOSTS

– clashing, smashing Chinese opera drums, cymbals and gongs, louder and louder as OLD SIX (as PILGRIM WARRIOR) takes centre stage in an open 'performance' space.

OLD SIX: *(As PILGRIM WARRIOR.)* '*I am Wu Song. Known as Pilgrim Warrior. I'm also known as Wu Song The Tiger Killer.*

*Because I killed a tiger. I fought many battles with our outlaw
fraternity of the marsh before we were granted amnesty by the
Song Emperor who enlisted our gallant band to put down a
grievous rebellion. We were surprised by this amnesty but those
in power often find use, in times of peril, for those they would
normally abjure.*

*Now on Armistice Day
Wu Song treads the golden way
To the court of the king
For a celebration song he never learned to sing
The circle took longer with no Miraculous Traveller.'*

Clack-clack-clack.

*BIG DOG enters as EMPEROR. They both process in an 'opera' circle
before they 'perform.' But more knowingly. With more sense of 'self.'*

*They pantomime seeing each other. OLD SIX as PILGRIM WARRIOR
kowtows to BIG DOG as EMPEROR.*

BIG DOG: *(As EMPEROR.)* *'Most brave Wu Song.'*

OLD SIX: *(As PILGRIM WARRIOR.)* *'Your most enlightened highness.
Emperor of all under heaven. Lord of Ten Thousand Years/'*

BIG DOG: *(As EMPEROR.)* *'You are alone, pilgrim?'*

OLD SIX: *(As PILGRIM WARRIOR.)* *'Highness, I left the Miraculous
Traveller. And I lost many brothers along the way.'*

BIG DOG: *(As EMPEROR.)* *'We feel grieved for your trial and loss.'*

OLD SIX: *(As PILGRIM WARRIOR.)* *'Majesty, because I am only a
crude talentless rustic, I can never repay your grace's kindness,
though I spill my liver and brains on the battlefield. Who
would've thought we would be depleted thus!'*

BIG DOG: *(As EMPEROR.)* *'We shall praise the deeds of those who
died or who are lost.*

Your service will not be Forgotten.'

OLD SIX: *(As PILGRIM WARRIOR; bows lower.)* *'Excellency!'*

BIG DOG: *(As EMPEROR.)* *'What reward may I grant you?'*

OLD SIX: *(As PILGRIM WARRIOR.)* *'That I can meditate and end my days quietly.'*

BIG DOG: *(As EMPEROR.)* *'Pilgrim, I can bestow on you silver and gold and women and silks and fine wine.'*

OLD SIX: *(As PILGRIM WARRIOR.)* *'The regime is corrupt, majesty. Narrow-hearted sycophants have your ear. They employ only their intimates. They reprove only their enemies.*

My humble apologies, majesty.'

BIG DOG: *(As EMPEROR.)* *'It is forgotten.'*

Clack-clack-clack.

Now they face front as OLD SIX and BIG DOG once again –

OLD SIX: The ghosts of our stage leave and arrive

BIG DOG: From the gate of ghosts at our stage's side

OLD SIX: Life and life's end on our stage inscribed

Clack-clack-clack.

OLD SIX: Our theatre brings those who are gone back to life.

BIG DOG: Our theatre is about those that never die.

OLD SIX: Now we exit through the gate of ghosts.

They turn and walk slowly upstage until they fade away.
As the sun rises, bright and shining…

10. EPILOGUE. IN PARIS, THE PROFESSOR ENCOUNTERS THE FUTURE OF CHINA WHICH HAS BEEN PAINTED OUT OF THE PICTURE

Paris in the spring time. Idyllic and serene.

THE PROFESSOR is sat on the street corner reading a newspaper. Facing him is a young woman, EMILIE TSCHENG.

PROFESSOR: *(Referring to the paper.)* This is unbelievable!

EMILIE: It's an ocean of bitterness is what it is!

PROFESSOR: The Japanese delegation demanded *racial equality*?

EMILIE: With real Five Tumuli bravado!

PROFESSOR: What would they hope to achieve by demanding *racial equality?*

EMILIE: The British and the French both have vast empires. The supposed good American brothers live segregated and superior to their former black slaves.

PROFESSOR: So rather than agree equality with we lowly races they'd prefer to sign a treaty gifting Shandong to Japan like a wedding dinner of roast hog.

EMILIE: It's not all though. One of our former premiers/–

PROFESSOR: Which one? I've lost track/

EMILIE: – had already signed secret treaties with the Japanese government in return for loans.

PROFESSOR: Wait. Loans from the Japanese???

EMILIE: The Japanese government has stated they'll return the Shandong territories in the future. But they won't say when.

PROFESSOR: Which means never.

EMILIE: One young man at Beijing University cut off his finger and wrote on the university wall in blood, demanding the return of the territories. There's protest everywhere. Riots, civil unrest, boycotts of Japanese goods/

PROFESSOR: And here in Paris?

EMILIE: Did you not hear? We blocked them in their fucking hotel. There was no way they were getting out of there to sign that bogus peace treaty.

PROFESSOR: I'm not used to hearing a woman swear.

EMILIE: Women can swear and fight just the same without fucking things up like men.

PROFESSOR: I have no doubt of that, Miss Tscheng/

EMILIE: Don't call me 'Miss Tscheng' like you're my father trying to palm me off on to some earnest white-eyed suitor/

PROFESSOR: Sorry. *Emilie.*

How many of you students are there here in Paris?

EMILIE: More all the time. Even in the midst of all the chaos at home they want us to learn in the West.

PROFESSOR: And are you art students the most radical?

EMILIE: My art has to carry the pain of our homeland in my brush strokes.

PROFESSOR: Pain is all we have. Humour is a thing for western dinner parties where even slaughter and segregation are treated as subjects for pleasantry.

EMILIE: Are you a writer?

PROFESSOR: I'm a schoolteacher. I just want to stay in Europe as long as I can.

EMILIE: Lucky you then, working for the French rather than those British. Though they've all fed their consciences to crows.

PROFESSOR: I was with the British actually.

EMILIE: Then how?

PROFESSOR: A very good friend of mine from a village in Shandong taught me: we Chinese all look alike. As long as someone turns up for work when the role call is made in the morning no one's fussed.

EMILIE: Your friend from the Shandong village sounds like the cow's cunt. Get him to join us.

PROFESSOR: He died. They both did. Clearing a battlefield. Unexploded bomb. So close to the end.

EMILIE: They won't die in vain.

PROFESSOR: Their names should be sung from the peaks of mountains.

EMILIE: I saw a storyteller from Shandong. A woman. Performing *Tales From The Marsh* all on her own.

PROFESSOR: Where?

EMILIE: She was on the harbour in Hong Kong. She changed the story. They were women-warriors. Women-warriors who'd been cast out or abandoned. Who were fleeing from the furnace of fate and the law. She sang and talked of change, revolution.

PROFESSOR: Did you know her name?

EMILIE: She called herself the 'miraculous traveller.'

PROFESSOR: Second Moon!

EMILIE: She said she wanted to come to France. I would've paid for her if I could.

PROFESSOR: Second Moon! Their opera song survives then. So their story will…

EMILIE: Story?

PROFESSOR: I thought at first I was educating them. It was they that educated me. Workers. That's what China has. The hardest workers in the world. Broken, abused and cast aside.

EMILIE: Things will change. Radical thought is spreading like fire across our land.

PROFESSOR: But to what end, Emilie? How much blood will we have to shed? How many times will we be betrayed and turn in on each other as we do now? For how much longer will we be forced to live like cannibals/?

EMILIE: Be of sound mood. It was a great thing you did. You and your fellow workers. Put us on the map at least. It's a beginning! They mentioned you in the peace conference.

PROFESSOR: *(Referring to the newspaper.)* On our 'day of sorrow' as our delegate Wellington Koo calls it here. He was the very picture of chalcedony cheer when he arrived four months ago. He even travelled here with the American president!

EMILIE: Come, let's walk. I want to show you the city properly. You've only just arrived and seen nothing.

They begin to walk, THE PROFESSOR limping.

PROFESSOR: It's true. All I've seen are mud and trenches with a bit of factory recently. The day they said 'you're moving to Paris to rebuild the city' I could have thanked all my ancestors on the spot.

EMILIE: You don't want to go back at all?

PROFESSOR: One day maybe.

They have come to a part of the stage where the lights go up on an ARTIST working on a huge mural painting. He wears a scarf that conceals his face.

What is this?

EMILIE: They're painting a giant picture to celebrate the war and all the peoples who participated in its winning. The biggest picture ever!

PROFESSOR: It's magnificent.

EMILIE: When socialism liberates our country from warlords and cliques do you think they'll commission me to paint big pictures by the heavenly gate?

PROFESSOR: Where are the Chinese?

EMILIE: What?

PROFESSOR: Where are we? I can't see us in this picture. Where are we?

EMILIE: That's...I can't see ei/ther –

PROFESSOR: We're not there/

EMILIE: Let me ask.

To the ARTIST in French:

Excuse me, sir. This mural depicts all the peoples who contributed in the entente war victory, yes?

ARTIST: *(French.)* Yes, that's the idea.

EMILIE: *(French.)* Why are there no Chinese in this picture? Our people worked behind the lines. Some of them died. Why are they not in the picture?

ARTIST: *(French.)* Oh that! They said there was no room for the Americans so they told us to paint over the Chinese with American faces.

EMILIE: Grandmother from your mother's side!

PROFESSOR: What did he say?

EMILIE: …

PROFESSOR: Emilie!

EMILIE: He said there was no room for the Americans so they were told to paint over the Chinese with American faces.

ARTIST: *(French.)* It's like putting cows' faces on horses heads or something.

PROFESSOR: No room?

EMILIE: That's what he said.

PROFESSOR: There were thousands and thousands of us and there's no room??

We dig and work and die and there's no room??

We pay for the mistakes of the powerful with our blood and there's no room??

ARTIST: *(French.)* Typical government bureaucrats. Know nothing of art and perspective!

EMILIE: *(To THE PROFESSOR.)* Try and be calm, brother, we can rectify this/ in time –

But THE PROFESSOR is confronting the ARTIST in rudimentary French –

PROFESSOR: *(To the artist in French.)* Where are the Chinese? Where are the Chinese???

ARTIST: *(French.)* What the hell –?

THE PROFESSOR has seized a big pot of red paint –

PROFESSOR: *(French.)* Where are they? Where are the Chinese??

ARTIST: *(French.)* I just told the girl, they made me paint over them, it's not my fault, I just do/ as I'm told –

PROFESSOR: *(French.)* WHERE ARE THE CHINESE???

ARTIST: *(French.)* What are you –? What are you doing?

With a scream of rage THE PROFESSOR flings the red paint at the mural screen where it splashes across the picture in a bloody red mess…

Silence.

EMILIE: *(Softly.)* Magnificent!

ARTIST: *(French.)* Bloody hell!

PROFESSOR: Gone. All gone.

The sound of the next sixty years or so of Chinese history rises slowly as the red paint runs. The sounds of chanting, of fury, of turmoil, of 'The East Is Red' and 'The Internationale'. It builds and builds before fading as the scene above does.

Then silence.

END.

Acknowledgements

Rikki Beadle Blair, John R Gordon, Alex Chang,
Andrew Koji, Samantha Joann, Shuang Teng, Lucy Sheen,
Steve Lau, Dr. Diana Yeh, Andrew Leung, Elizabeth Chan,
Siu Hun Li, Matthew Leonhart, Rikki Henry, Jade Lewis,
Jane Gibson, Petra Hjortsberg, Kerry Michael, Karen Fisher,
Theatre Royal Stratford East, Dr. Ross Forman, Paul French,
Mark O' Neill, Frances Wood, Professor Nicholas Saunders,
Professor Paul Bailey, Yen Chan, East London Chinese
Community Centre, Katie Leung, Colin Ryan, Richard Rees,
Jonathan Raggett, Dr. Anne Witchard, Nic Wass, Claire Birch,
RSC Other Place, Nina Steiger, Gillian Greer, Sonny Leong,
Andrew Hughes, ETT, Nicole Miners, Martin Sarreal,
Dan Li, James Cooney, Hannah Bevan, Katy Snelling,
NST City Southampton, Annelie Powell, Peng Wenlan,
Fin Kennedy, Daniel Harrison, Theatre Royal Plymouth,
Arts Council England, Pete Staves, Wei Ming Kam,
Serena Grasso, Oberon Books, all *The Good Immigrant*
writers especially Nikesh Shukla, British East
Asian Artists, BEATS org.

And all who've participated in the fight for better
representation for British East Asians in UK media,
you know who you are and you know who you're not.